COMMUNICATION

EMERGENCE, EVOLUTION AND ITS PROGRESSION INTO NEWSPAPERS

DR. VIJAY BHASKAR

INDIA · SINGAPORE · MALAYSIA

ISBN 979-8-89744-673-5

Dedicated To

Aryan & Adhrit

For keeping me live and productive during difficult times

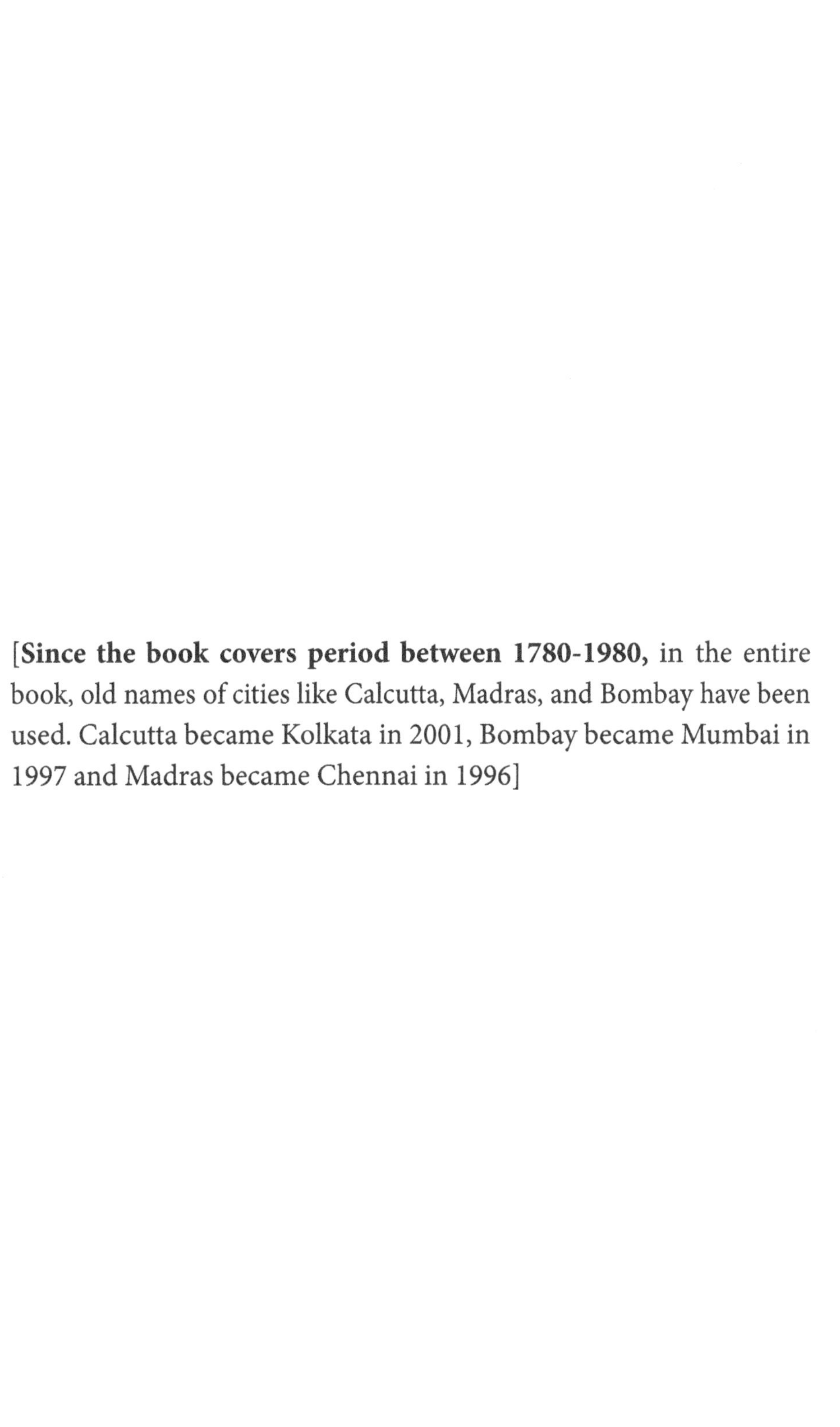

[**Since the book covers period between 1780-1980,** in the entire book, old names of cities like Calcutta, Madras, and Bombay have been used. Calcutta became Kolkata in 2001, Bombay became Mumbai in 1997 and Madras became Chennai in 1996]

Contents

Acknowledgment

A hardcore journalist would tempt to agree with German Sociologist Max Weber, who, in a lecture at Munich, said, "Not everyone realizes that to write a good piece of journalism, at least is as demanding intellectually as the achievement of any scholar..." It is true since a piece of journalism is produced impromptu and is supposed to make an impact. Even though produced under entirely different conditions (from scholarly research), one overlooks that a journalist's actual responsibility is far higher than that of the scholar.

The book traces gradual progress in science and technology that gave rise to newspapers opening the door for public domination of knowledge. But, it was the innate human desire to communicate that necessitated the related inventions, and the entire communication technology is an extension of this basic human desire. The book picks up from the cause that made humans speak in the first place and from there to different stages of communication finally leading to mass media, in this case, the newspapers.

It wasn't easy for me to organize my thoughts into a book. During a chance meeting with Prof. (Dr) Panchanan Mishra, an eminent historian, and after that, a few regular ones, the topic of the book was born. His intellectual rarity and infectious enthusiasm, despite his age, could put anyone to stretch extra miles. And I took up the responsibility even after my busy schedule of a Resident Editor. Pancha Baboo, as he was affectionately known, put me on the track initially, briefed me on how to start, and handed me over to one of his most trusted lieutenants, Prof. (Dr) Surendra Jha, Head, Department of History, SKM University,

Dumka, Jharkhand. For the entire period of the writing of this book, these two guides have been my real lighthouses of inspiration.

The post-internet era has made documentation and availability of information much more accessible It has speeded up news delivery to an astonishing level. But unlimited space and scope of this magical platform allow many corners from where confusion or misinformation could easily creep in. This is more evident today when mass media has another responsibility of slaying Fake News flooded by social media platforms. News delivery speed will further go up as far as science and technology will take it to. With continued development in the field yet further vehicle may be invented which can take humanity to still uncharted territories. Who knows!

The best part of this technology is that we can quite easily see India's first newspaper *Hicky's Gazette* aesthetically preserved digitally in Heidelberg University, Germany, or the report preserved in microfilms that forms part of the Indian newspaper Reports in the British Library, London. These all are illuminating, and so is the University of California site that has digitally recorded and preserved activities of the Pacific Coast Hindustan Association and their publication *Ghadar*.

We see a steady rise in the growth of the Indian press after 1857. Due to various restrictions, technologies were slow to make inroads in India. *The Statesman* was the first to use steam power to print newspapers in India. *The Hindu* has many firsts to its credit in acquiring the latest technologies in the printing of papers. The Indian press matured technologically from mid20th century onwards. The *Times of India, The Statesman, Hindustan Times* and *The Hindu,* were technologically capable of delivering newspapers that could easily compare with the excellent newspapers of the world. The same improvement was seen in vernacular newspapers in the north, south, east and west. Since then, Indian newspapers have been marching ahead and have turned many barren lands into thriving newspaper business centers.

I want to register my thanks to Shri Suman Kumar Singh – Correspondent, *Hindustan*, Dumka, for his immense help. He was always a dependable colleague of mine during my editorship at Bhagalpur, Bihar, and is still so reliable.

During its final draft, for months, my study room was cluttered with pages of manuscript, power-on computer terminals, and other related systems. These papers were neatly arranged in the morning so that I could start my work afresh. This rearrangement was done by my wife Ms. Asha Singh. I will remain indebted to her for her help. My son Abhishek, Abhinav, and daughters-in-laws Priya and Neha also deserve mention as they eagerly awaited the completion of the work, this prompted me to come out of my chronic indolence and finish the book.. Also, my mother was in Ranchi during the completion of the project and I am hugely humbled for her blessings. I also want to register my thanks to Sri Y N Singh, who is a guardian, guide, and philosopher to me for the last four decades. As head of a large family, he always encourages me and everyone else to keep doing what they are capable of. I am also thankful to my close friend Dharmaraj Rai, whom I lost last year. He was a senior journalist of Ranchi and a colleague for many reasons.

It took a long time to schedule the publication of the book. Corona time (from March 2020 onwards) provided an opportunity to revise the draft, but it also delayed the publication.

Now, let me introduce to you the efficient team which worked tirelessly in the background leading the way from the raw manuscript to its final destination. I am grateful to Sunayna Choradiya: my publishing consultant, Hamza Namatkar: pre-publishing manager, Arputha, Akanksha and Sarvesh: publishing managers, Sanhita Sinha: editor, Kevis Tech: Typesetter and John Jasso who made the cover-these are all professionals from Notion Press to whom I will remain indebted.

Jitendra Poddar has been my constant companion for the last couple of years, and he helped in keying the manuscript. Arun working with me as a designer has worked on the photographs of the book. Shailendra, a promising mass comm student of mine and a working journalist helped me indexing the book.

The first draft was seen by Ms. Sonali Das, a colleague and senior journalist with The Times of India, Ranchi establishment. I am grateful to her. Prof. Ashok Priyadarshi, Dr. B K Mishra and Dr. G K Singh of Ranchi University, Sri Vijaydutt Sridhar of Sapre Sangrhalaya, Bhopal, and journalist and colleague Sri Harish Pathak of Mumbai who provided much- needed help in the final phase.

Though the book touches development of newspapers around the world, the focus of the book is Indian newspapers published from 1780-1980. I'd to restrict myself to a period of 200 years and one medium i.e. newspapers. I did not want to make canvas too large to be handled deftly or things were thrown off gear.

– Vijay Bhaskar
Ranchi.

Prologue

When we see from a historical point of view, mass media communication is a recent development. Printing of books, newspapers, magazines, journals, etc., and their mass circulation became possible only because of the development in science and technology. The invention of movable type, and later printing, was a landmark beginning that pushed the world into the real Information Age. It was due to the invention of new scientific tools and technologies that the Industrial Revolution took place in the West, and that led to manifold development. The rise of an educated middle class necessitated the demand for published, printed materials on various aspects of human needs. The development of mass media was supplemented further by a large number of means of communication such as railways, telegraphs, telephones, and various means of road transport as well.

Mass media communication, however, is a vast subject, and therefore, the present work has put special emphasis on development in science and technology that made publishing newspapers possible. Right from the beginning, newspapers have hugely impacted society in ways more than one. The cost of newspapers suited every pocket, brought the goings-on of the world before its readers every morning, changed the narrative of public discourse forever, and for the first time, paved the way for an inclusive mindset. Though the period of work formally begins from 1780 when the first newspaper in India *Bengal Gazette* or *The Original Calcutta General Advertiser* saw the light of the day. I have pulled back a bit, the same way as an archer pulls the string of the bow back to focus more accurately on the target ahead. Hence, nature's exclusive gift to species of *Homo sapiens*, which made the speech possible in the first place, has been briefly covered. This single anatomical feature pushed the entire humanity's communication ability into a much higher orbit. Perhaps, it was this necessity that was the moving force behind invention in science and technology that made newspapers a reality. The parallel development of writing and writing materials is discussed to maintain the continuity of the subject. The effort put in by humanity to prepare handwritten record of activities before the advent of printing is amazing. Nature's exclusive gift, as well as recording information in antiquity – both have been covered under the role of science and technology in the rise and growth of mass media. The period of study ends in 1980. It covers a time span of 200 years.

We see two prevalent cultures before the print culture: Oral culture and scribe culture. Oral culture, also called traditional culture, is called so because in traditional societies, knowledge transfer was done by this mode from one generation to another.

Oral tradition had been an integral part of societies around the world. The Vedic traditions, Buddha's *Udana* (utterance), Mahavir's *Vani* (Speech) and Muhammad Sahib's *Hadith* have all come down to us orally. The Meos, living mostly in Mewat, have kept their culture alive through the oral traditions. However, as society developed, the written word became an effective tool of communication as well as a great source for gathering news. News-gathering was perfected as an intelligentsia organization of great administrative and political significance particularly under Kautilya of *Arthasastra* fame. Asoka, who ruled in 3rd century BCE. used pillar and rock edicts to communicate his thoughts on ethics and morals to his subjects. Messages were also at times couriered by pigeons, and one must not fail to mention that Kalidasa invoked the cloud above in the sky to send his message to reach his lady love, far away from him, revealing his extremely rich imagination in depicting the landscape, topography, the social and cultural condition of the people living on the routes of the message. It is indeed a unique reality and invites researchers to discover the Indian way of life.

News-gathering continued during the Muslim Rule in India. Gazanavi dynasty, which established its rule over Punjab, had a system of NEWS collection that was a source of intelligence about the princes and plutocrats of the neighboring areas, the cause of battles and the personal lives of generals.

Though news gathering and news-carriers were part of the administrative and military intelligence system under the first two Mughal emperors, it was under Akbar the Great that the organization of news expanded into an effective agency. There were also private newsletters written by newsagents employed by merchants.

Historians agree that Akbar picked up many crucial keys to better governance from that of the famous ruler of the short-lived Afghan dynasty (1540-1547) Sher Shah Suri (born 1486, Sasaram, Bihar, died March 22, 1545, in Kalinjar). Sher Shah Suri deeply involved himself in developing communication infrastructure for the empire. Perhaps he knew it well that communication was the key to holding the empire intact. He finished the longest road project of the time, the Grand Trunk Road, popularly known as G T Road, spanning over 2500 km (1600 miles), connecting Chittagong in the east (now in Bangladesh) to Kabul (Afghanistan) in the west via Agra and Delhi. The road is still in existence and has been taken in the Indian National Highway System. He laid the foundation of the national postal system. Excellent improvement in new road networks in north India facilitated all his administrative reforms and postal services.

Meanwhile, India came into contact with European merchants. The first to come were the Portuguese. Vasco Da Gama reached Calicut in 1498. Gradually the Dutch, the French and the British traders became involved in a war among themselves for supremacy with the help of local chieftains. It is interesting to note that the Portuguese attended the court of Akbar and presented him two significant gifts – a miniature printing press and a navy. Akbar, however, ignored the significance of these gifts and failed to develop a printing press and a naval force, and according to the great historian Nihar Ranjan Ray, this negligence ultimately led to the downfall of the Mughal Empire in India. However, the point is debatable. Akbar sought the help of Ottomans, and also increasingly of Europeans (especially Portuguese and Italians) in procuring firearms and artillery. The Portuguese remained confined to Goa, where they established the first printing press in India. It was used for religious purposes only.

The period of study is divided into the pre- and post-Gutenberg era. Gutenberg's invention of movable type was an epoch-making invention that led to the proliferation of the printing press and made the publication of newspapers possible, thus putting the unprecedented stamp of mass media. But it wasn't that pre-Gutenberg world lived in a stultified silence.

The art of printing and paper-making was first put into fairly wide use by the Chinese in the 2nd century CE The Chinese were first to develop ink, paper and the movable type, and they brought the first newspaper on silk. It reached India via Europe after the 14th century. By the middle of the 17th century, printing was a common phenomenon in Europe and North America. However, the earliest known journalistic effort was the handwritten *Acta Diuerna* (Daily Doings or Journal of the Day) of the 1St century CE in Rome. The earliest newspaper is supposed to be *aller Fürnemmen und gedenckwürdigen Historien* (Account of all distinguished and memorable news) known as *Relation* published by a German publisher Johann Carolus (1575–1634) from Strasburg, France. The other newspaper of notable importance was The *Frankfurter Zeitung*, a German-language newspaper that appeared from 1856 to 1943. The first English newspaper was the *Weekly News* (1622–41), and one of the earliest daily publications in England was the *Daily Courante*, which began its publication in 1702. In the USA, the first newspaper was *Public Occurrences*, a news sheet published for just one issue in Boston in 1690. The earliest continuous publication was the *Boston Newsletter*, established in 1704. Journalism became an established activity in Europe and America by the first decade of the 18th century. The publication of newspapers got an upward thrust

(1) Numb. 1.

The Oxford Gazette.

Publiſhed by Authority.

Oxon. Nov. 7.

This day the Reverend Dr. *Walter Blandford*, Warden of *Wadham Colledge* in this Univerſity, was Elected Lord Biſhop of this See, vacant by the death of Dr. *Paul*, late Biſhop here.

Oxon. Nov. 12. This day His Majeſty in Councel, according to the uſual cuſtom, having the Roll of Sheriffs preſented to him, pricked theſe perſons following to be Sheriffs for the ſucceeding Year, in their reſpective Counties of *England* and *Wales*.

Berks.	Baſil Brent, *Eſquire.*
Bedford.	Tho: Snagge, *Eſq;*
Buckingham.	Simon Bennet, *Eſq;*
Cumberland.	Sir William Dalſton, *Baronet.*
Cheſter.	Sir John Ardegne, *Knight.*
Cambridge.	Sir Tho: Willis, *Kt. and Baronet.*
Cornwal.	Tho: Dorrel, *Eſq;*
Devon.	John Kelland, *Eſq;*
Dorſet.	Roger Clavel, *Eſq;*

ſieur *de Canillac* having been put to death by the Commiſſioners of the *Grands Iours*: It ſeems they had laid ſome new Taxes or Impoſitions on thoſe parts: There are Troups marching againſt them, and it is thought they will ſoon be reduced. My Lord *Aubigny* Lord *Almoner* to her Majeſty, having layen ſick ſome time here of an Hydropſie attended with a Flux, is this week dead.

Paris Novemb: 18. The *Mareſchal de Turenne* arrived here on Sunday laſt from the Frontiers, whence he brings account that the Succors intended againſt the Prince of *Munſter* had paſſed in ſmall parties, and that they had been received at *Maeſtricht* by *Monſieur Beverning* in the name of the States General.

Guernzy, Octob. 30. Yeſterday came into our Road the *Unity* Frigot, Captain *Trafford* Commander, who brought in a Prize Captain *Iohn Gilſon* of *Fluſhing*, being a Privateer of 7 Guns, and 45 Men.

Chattham Nov. 4. Captain *Eliot* Commander of the *Saphire* has taken 3 Buſſes, two of them out of 50 at the *Dogger-ſands*, under the Protection of four of their Men of War. In his paſſage home, tis ſaid, he ſaw ſeveral tops

Numb.

The Daily Courant.

Wedneſday, March 11. 1702.

From the Harlem Courant, Dated March 18. N. S.

Naples, Feb. 22.

ON Wedneſday laſt, our New Viceroy, the Duke of Eſcalona, arriv'd here with a Squadron of the Galleys of Sicily. He made his Entrance dreſt in a French habit; and to give us the greater Hopes of the King's coming hither, went to Lodge in one of the little Palaces, leaving the Royal one for his Majeſty. The Marquis of Grigni is alſo arriv'd here with a Regiment of French.

Rome, Feb. 25. In a Military Congregation of State hat was held here, it was Reſolv'd to draw a Line rom Aſcoli to the Borders of the Eccleſiaſtical State, ereby to hinder the Incurſions of the Tranſalpine roops. Orders are ſent to Civita Vecchia to fit out e Galleys, and to ſtrengthen the Garriſon of that ace. Signior Caſali is made Governor of Perugia. he Marquis del Vaſto, and the Prince de Caſerta ntinue ſtill in the Imperial Embaſſador's Palace; ere his Excellency has a Guard of 50 Men every

Flanders under the Duke of Burgundy; and the Duke of Maine is to Command upon the Rhine.

From the Amſterdam Courant, Dated Mar. 18.

Rome, Feb. 25. We are taking here all poſſible Precautions for the Security of the Eccleſiaſtical State in this preſent Conjuncture, and have deſir'd to raiſe 3000 Men in the Cantons of Switzerland. The Pope has appointed the Duke of Berwick to be his Lieutenant-General, and he is to Command 6000 Men on the Frontiers of Naples: He has alſo ſettled upon him a Penſion of 6000 Crowns a year during Life.

From the Paris Gazette, Dated Mar. 18. 1702.

Naples, Febr. 17. 600 French Soldiers are arrived here, and are expected to be follow'd by 3400 more. A Courier that came hither on the 14th. has brought Letters by which we are aſſur'd that the King of Spain deſigns to be here towards the end of March; and accordingly Orders are given to make the ne-

The first issue of Oxford Gazette, and the first British daily newspaper The Daily Courant, dated March 11, 1702. Photo credit: The Story of Journalism by Elizabeth Grey, Longmans Young Books, London & Harlow, 1968 edition. page 25.

owing to the birth of a new middle class. The middle class was the product of the Industrial Revolution that had necessitated the social, economic and political changes, which in turn depended hugely on easy means of communication to organize themselves and also to quench the thirst for knowledge. However, no such change took place in the East as there was no Renaissance or Industrial Revolution to propel such growth. The feudal system was prevalent everywhere. The first printed newspaper in the East was probably produced from wooden blocks in Peking (now Beijing) in between 7th and 8th century CE. But printing did not catch up with the imagination of the people. Learning was still the prerogative of the priestly class, and information was preserved on palm leaves in many parts of Asia, including India. In India *Bhrigu Samhita* in original is still available preserved on palm leaves. Even during the time of Akbar, Tulsidas wrote *Ramcharitamanas* on palm leaves only, and it is still available in original with a priest of a temple in Chitrakoot.

The first newspaper was published in 1780 in the English language by J.A. Hicky. After that, several newspapers published from Calcutta, Madras and Bombay (altogether 13 in number) came into being by the end of the 18th century. These newspapers mainly addressed Company employees, and contents were largely insignificant from a common man's point of view. With the abolition of the trade monopoly of the East India Company in 1813, many business houses came to India, and they supported the publication of newspapers that could serve their trade and commerce. As such, James Silk Buckingham edited *Calcutta Journal* in 1818 and a new era of Anglo-Indian journalism began, which was a new kind of commercial journalism that disseminated news of general interest as well. Another remarkable feature was the publication of journals in various Indian languages, and the lead was taken up by the Baptist Mission who brought out *Dig Darshan* in Bengali in 1818. By the end of the 19th century, newspapers and periodicals in almost all major Indian languages appeared. It is significant to note that none of the newspapers brought any news about the storm that had been brewing due to the rampant economic, political, social and cultural exploitation of the East India Company. The exploitation resulted in the Indian Mutiny of 1857, hailed as India's First War of Independence. There was also no mention of Santhal Uprising in 1855–56 which pre- staged the Mutiny of 1857. Later on, Motilal Nehru, Bal Gangadhar Tilak, Gopal Krishna Gokhale and G. Subrahmanyam Iyer started their newspapers to advocate the Indian nationalist cause. But the newspaper had not become a medium of communication as yet. The total number of newspapers circulating in the mid-19th century in India was about 3000, and the major share was that of newspapers run by the British.

The appearance of Mahatma Gandhi brought a qualitative paradigm change in Indian newspapers. Gandhi protested against the Rowlatt Act and Jallianwala Bagh massacre, and launched Satyagraha against British authority. Gandhi's peaceful resistance, civil disobedience and non-cooperation got wide coverage in the Indian newspapers. Gandhi himself started the publication of *Young India, Navjeevan* and *Harijan,* and converted the press into a powerful instrument of public opinion, building on political, economic, social and cultural consequences of British rule in India. Gandhi, however, did not like the use of media for popular entertainment or for making money. He considered the media to be a powerful force that should serve the welfare of the society and should never be (mis) used for money-making.

The role played by authors like Bankim Chandra, Rabindranath Tagore, Premchand, and poets like Maithili Sharan Gupta, Makhanlal Chaturvedi, Suvadra Kumari Chouhan and Ramdhari Singh Dinkar in India's freedom movement cannot be ignored. However, after independence, the Indian press grew into a profit-centric industry. Therefore, the Government appointed a Press Commission in 1952. There have been attempts to enlist newsmakers in the pre- and post-independent era. An exhaustive list is given in the appendix of this study; however, the list is not complete (and it cannot be as it is endless).

India greatly inherited the legacy of the British press, both technologically and intellectually. The legacy continued for quite long. The Indian press followed the same pattern of development, but along the way, they strayed much further from its real aims and objectives, and hence, another Press Commission was appointed by the Government in 1978. The Commission resigned and was reconstituted in 1980. It submitted its report in 1982.

After that, the nature and objectives of journalism changed and may be regarded as development-oriented, as that became an essential objective of developing countries like India.

Another mode of mass communication was movies that became possible owing to scientific and technological inventions of that time. By 1940, Bombay, Madras, and Calcutta were producing significant number of movies representing socially relevant themes.

The broadcast media had also started in 1927, which later on came under state control and came to be known as All India Radio. By 1947, there were eleven radio stations, and the number kept on growing. By 1978 there were 18 million receiver sets in India. Programs were relayed not only for entertainment but also for the economic, social, agricultural and general welfare of people.

Television came to India only in 1959 and was used for education, health and sanitation purposes, besides entertainment. Indian television's initial focus was agriculture, and one of its iconic programme *Krishi Darshan* (that still continues) became famous for educating farmers. In the entertainment segment, *Chitrahaar* – based on songs from movies – became immensely popular. Some daily soap operas also made their entry later.

Emergency imposed on the country in 1975 was like a litmus test for Indian press, which having fought a foreign power and being highly instrumental in making India a free country, suddenly found its freedom of speech entirely suspended by its own elected Government. It is interesting to see that the same sort of tools and techniques were used to gag the press that were used under an autocratic foreign rule.

Freedom of speech and expression is the core around which the structure of a firm democracy is interwoven. The way Indian press, barring a few, reacted to the restriction imposed by the Government, one is inclined to infer that emergency put Indian press on a trajectory that was not going to dock precisely with the idea of the absolute freedom of speech and expression.

1 Science and Technology Behind the Rise and Growth of Communication That Made Mass Media Possible

The role of science and technology in the rise and growth of mass media in India or anywhere else in the world has a few basic common elements. At every stage of human evolution, science and technology has played a key role in the development of tools and techniques to record information. Before that, much of the information present in the society existed in the oral matrix. In traditional societies, much of the learning was passed orally from one generation to the other. In India there was the concept of *Guru*[*] and his position in the society was the highest. Then writing and subsequently printing developed. Printing was the turning point in the development of human society as it opened the gate for public domination of knowledge, and ultimately paved the way for mass media. With every successive medium, quantum of knowledge increased exponentially. Thus, whatever volume we had in the oral matrix was hugely surpassed by the written matrix, and whatever knowledge we had in the written matrix was hugely surpassed by the printed matrix, and whatever we have in the printed matrix, that was surpassed by audio-video matrix – the next stage of the development. And certainly, when we reached hyper-text medium,

* *गुरुर्ब्रह्मा गुरुर्विष्णु गुरुर्देवो महेश्वरः। गुरुः साक्षत् परं ब्रह्म तस्मै श्री गुरवे नमः।। Guru Brahma – Guru is Brahma, who is the Lord of Creation, also called as Generator, Guru Vishnu means Guru is Vishnu (Vishnu is the Lord who is called organizer), Guru Devo Maheshwarah means Guru is the Maheshwara (Shiva or the destroyer), Guru Saakshaat Parabrahma means, Guru is Parbrahma, i.e., the supreme god or almighty.*

quantum of knowledge altogether reached a new height. Science and technology of mass media developed in the West and was subsequently imported to India when it came in contact with the Portuguese and later, the British East India Company. The field of media saw hectic activities after the invention of the movable metal type and printing machine in Germany in 15th century. Gutenberg's remarkable machine was so perfect that the concept behind it remained unchanged for 500 years till the arrival of computers in the 20th century. It was the single invention of far-reaching consequences that gave the stamp of mass media for the first time and opened the gate for public domination of knowledge which had, to a great extent, been the prerogative of the elite class in the societies all over the world. Public domination of knowledge changed many things, but the foremost was change in the general psyche from an attitude of cold indifference to equal participation in governance. Any type of mass media is essentially an extension of the basic human desire to communicate. Humans are uniquely positioned in the Animal Kingdom having unmatched communication skills. Science and technology tell us that we owe this unique ability to a single anatomical feature known as the hyoid bone that really kicked our communication abilities in to a higher orbit. But it should not be construed that the world, including India, lay in stultified silence before the printing began. There was strong "oral culture" and the "scribe culture"; though none of these forms made mass media possible. Today we are simply amazed by the amount of labour and aesthetics that were put in to prepare a written document as science and technology has unearthed. There were so many processes that helped recording information in antiquity, but the story really began with the hyoid bone.

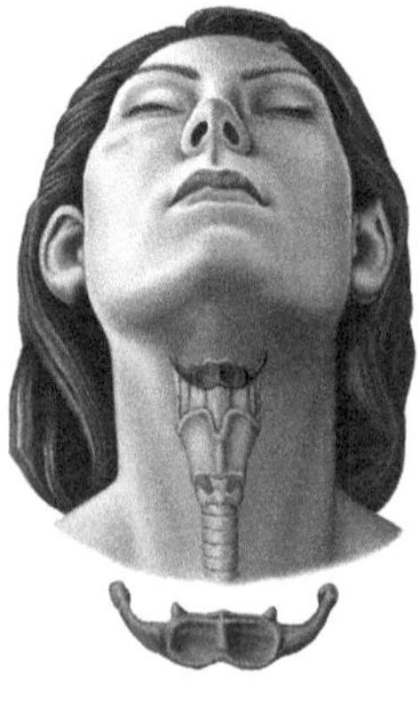

Hyoid Bone and Human's Ability to Communicate: Humans are gifted by nature with some anatomical features that is exclusive to the species and give it immense capacity to render complex speech. That is hyoid bone – a small horseshoe-shaped bone suspended in the muscles of our neck, like a piece of fruit trapped in Jell-O.

The hyoid bone is the only bone in the body that is not connected to any other bone. It is the foundation of speech and is found only in humans and Neanderthals in perfect position to render complex speech. Other animals have versions of the hyoid, but only the human variety is in the right position to work in unison with the larynx (the voice box) and the tongue, and make us the chatterboxes of the animal world. Without it, we'd still garble and hoot much like our chimpanzee cousins, scientists say. Scientist do believe that bipedalism helped humans to stand erect that facilitated the re-positioning of the hyoid bone and larynx in such a way that it made speech possible and it also helped in the development of the brain itself.

Studies based on discoveries of ancient hyoids indicate that humans likely had the capability to speak similar to the way we do today nearly 300,000 years ago. Alongside the hyoid, another important anatomical change happened around the same time that really kicked speaking into high gear – the larynx drop[2]. In human infants, the larynx sits up high in the nasal cavity like a snorkel so babies can drink and breathe at the same time. But, around three months of age, the larynx "drops" much lower in the throat, making choking easier but speech possible (the register of male voices lowers when the larynx drops again slightly during puberty). No other animal has a larynx low enough to produce sounds as complex as our ancient ancestors did and as we do today, including our close relatives, the chimpanzees, whose hyoid bone sits just a little too high to do anything but hoot and grunt.

The first words came from *Homo heidelbergensis*[*] – the species of early human roaming the earth when our anatomy changed to allow complex speech. *Heidelbergensis* – believed to be related to both modern humans

---

* *Homo heidelbergensis is known to have lived from at least 600,000 years ago in Africa and Europe to maybe as late as 250,000 years ago in some areas.*

and Neanderthals, – probably wasn't Shakespeare- eloquent on his first try, but it wasn't long before people were chatting up a storm.[2] As soon as speech became anatomically possible, putting sounds together into a clear structure that everyone could understand became advantageous, anthropologists agree. This process is called the language.

Complex speech meant individuals could share ideas and concepts like never before. It's no coincidence, say anthropologists, that we see the first hints of culture around this time as well.

Neanderthals whose hyoid and larynx are almost identical to early modern humans, started to show signs of symbolism and religion about 100,000 years ago, by burying their dead with grave offerings. Art and music followed soon after.[3] Neanderthal speech likely had fewer vowels and consonants due to the restrictive shape of their nasal cavity, adapted for living in cold climates.

Just that little disadvantage may have led to the demise of the Neanderthals as opposed to our chat-happy ancestors, some experts say.[4]

It is a commonplace of sociological doctrine that man as a social being exists in and through communication; communication is as basic to man's nature as is hunger for food.[5]

Humans had been speaking for a couple of hundred thousand years before they got the inspiration or nerve to mark their ideas down for posterity. But when Mesopotamian people (the Sumerians) finally did scratch out a few book-keeping symbols on clay tablets 5,000 years ago, they unknowingly started a whole new era in history. Sumerians were first to record a message that was not in the form of a picture.[6,7] The presence of written sources denotes the technical dividing line between what scholars classify as prehistory versus what they call history, which starts at different times depending on what part of the world you're studying in. In most places, writing started about the same time that ancient civilizations emerged from hunter- gatherer communities, probably as a way to keep track of the new concept of "property", such as animals, grain supplies or when land writing started.

By 3000 BCE in Mesopotamia (present-day Iraq), and then soon after in Egypt, and by 1500 BCE, in China, people were scribbling, sketching and talking about their world, about their culture in a very permanent way.[8]

When ancient Mesopotamians started settling down in farms surrounding the first cities, life became a bit more complicated. Agriculture required expertise and detailed record-keeping – two elements that led directly to the invention of writing, historians say. The first examples of writing were pictograms used by temple officials to keep track of the inflows and outflows of the city's grain and animal stores which, in the bigger Sumerian urban centers, were big enough to make counting by memory unreliable. Officials began using standardized symbols rather than, say, an actual picture of a goat to represent commodities, scratched into soft clay tablets with a pointed reed that had been cut into a wedge shape. Archaeologists call this first writing "cuneiform" from the Latin *cuneus*, meaning wedge.[9] The system developed quickly to incorporate signs that represented sounds, and soon all of Mesopotamia was taking notes, making to-do lists, etc. Egyptian writing – the famous hieroglyphics – developed independently not long thereafter under similar circumstances, historians think.[10] A couple of thousand years later, as variations on the two systems spread throughout the region, the entire ancient world had writing schemes that vastly improved the efficiency of economies, the accountability of Governments and, maybe most importantly to us, our understanding of the past.

Reading and writing in ancient times weren't for the masses. However, daily life in Mesopotamia and Egypt was time-consuming, and so writing became a specialized profession, usually for members of the elite class. The highly regarded scribes of ancient Mesopotamia were even depicted in art, wearing cuneiform-writing implements (a bit like a set of chopsticks) in their belts as a mark of their importance. Literacy remained a privilege of aristocratic males in most societies of the world all the way until the 19th century, when public education became more widespread.

It means that while the historical period is exponentially better understood than the experiences of humans before writing was invented, written accounts are largely about the experiences of the upper classes, historians say. "The modern alphabet was evolved by Romans and brought to Western Europe at the time of Roman Empire, roughly about 2000 years ago."[11]

The invention of writing, and in particular of alphabetic writing, marked a milestone in cultural development. It provided humanity with a new means of communication that literally inscribed spoken word in stone and broke the barriers of time and space. Space because writing could be sent from one place to another and time because it could be preserved for generations to come.

Means of Recording Information in Antiquity: Since the discovery of writing, nearly every form of writing has been tried and tested. Some were expensive, having longer life; others were inexpensive but temporary in nature. From wax notepad to grandeur of monumental inscription in stone, almost everything we know about antiquity is derived from writing, such as those written on plant product or animal skin or on metals.

Excavation at Pompeii* indicates that pads (thin wooden boards with a fine coating of beeswax) were in use. Writing in wax was possible with use of stylus. A stylus used to be sharp at one end and broader at the other. The term "literacy style" is related to this stylus. Stone and metal (copper sheets and bronze tablets) were used in ancient Rome that contained detail about treatise and decrees. Royal houses sometimes used silver and gold.

---

* *The city of Pompeii was an ancient Roman town-city near modern Naples in the Italian region of Campania.*

Writing materials that form part of the antiquity are:

Stone: Stone was a kind of a natural choice for writing as well as carving due to its availability and hardened surface. It was mainly used for writing on permanent monuments and public buildings. It is also the oldest form of writing. Writing on stone usually required the use of hammer and chisel. The most comfortable, accurate, and hence, productive manner of carving stone inscriptions is to hold the chisel in one hand and hit it with the hammer held in the other hand.

Although this sounds like too simple an explanation, one must consider that as most people are right-handed then there would be a tendency to cut the letters from right to left. "Therefore, we find that the flow of ancient Semitic languages such as Hebrew and Arabic run from right to left."[12]

Metal: Sheets of metal were rarely used for writing or are rarely found. For one, they were expensive to manufacture and secondly, the metal was often re-smelted for use as weapons in times of war, so few sheets remain. Royal houses sometimes used silver or gold and examples of writing on gold has been excavated from the Second temple period in Jerusalem.* More commonly, bronze tablets and copper sheets were used to provide semi-permanence and could be stored more easily than cumbersome rock. Archaeologists have discovered row-upon-row of bronze tablets from ancient Roman archives that contain details about treaties and decrees. Soldiers honorably discharged from serving in the Roman Army were given a small bronze tablet with their right as citizen recorded on it. These were known as diplomas and we derive modern academic graduation from this source.

Wood: The use of wood as a writing medium was strictly confined to temporary purposes and not many such tablets have survived the test

* *The Second Temple Period refers to the city of Jerusalem (the principal city of Judea) during the period from 538 BCE to 70 CE.*

of time as the climate in most countries was not conducive to their preservation. Apart from some well-preserved palm wood found in Buddhist libraries in the East, the only good source of timber tablets is in the dry sands of Egypt, where the flooding Nile could not reach.

In antiquity, wooden boards were used for displaying public announcements. The Romans called them albums. They were whitened boards and when the message became out of date the board could easily be whitewashed and rewritten. The qualities of slaves would be written on such boards and they would be made to stand under them while being paraded for sale.[13]

Wax: An extremely temporary method of writing was to scratch the record onto wax tablets. These were thin wooden boards covered with a fine coating of beeswax. The boards could have small holes at one end that permitted a ring to be inserted allowing many sheets to form a flip book. The Latin name for this was *codex* and has become common in referring to any group of bound pages.

Wax pads were often used as notebooks. At Pompeii, excavations have shown that even contracts as important as banking or loans were recorded on wax tablets. This may have been a quick, temporary method prior to a more permanent one, much like a secretary making shorthand notes before typing them up. School students used the wax tablet as a writing notepad. Once the information was learned, the tablet could be smoothed clean for reuse.

The wax note pads were written on using a sharp stylus. Pads of two or three leaves were called diptychs or triptychs.

Ostraca: These are broken shreds of pottery that have writing scratched onto them. Being basically useless, potshards were discarded. However, as they were made of fired clay, they were very hard and almost indestructible, thus used as writing material.

Clay Tablets: Clay tablets are probably the invention of the Sumerians of southern Babylonia. The use of soft clay tablets was popular right up to until the Christian era. Use of clay tablets became widespread and was the general means of written communication throughout Mesopotamia and the entire ancient East.[14] The system of use involved two parts: the tablet proper that was fashioned as a letter and formed the inner core of the communication. Shrouding the inner tablet was a folded clay "envelope" that completely enclosed the inner tablet. The message to be sent was first written on the smaller, inner tablet. It was made of soft clay and a thin, sharpened tool was used to inscribe wedge-shaped uniform letters that comprised the text. This tablet was then fired to harden it and make the message permanent.

It was then wrapped in a thin sheet of clay that was folded around the main message like a modern envelope. This was inscribed with the name of the recipient, the contents of the inner tablet and the name (and possibly the seal) of the author.

These tablets have been excavated by the thousand from archaeological sites all over the East. There are at least one million tablets held and displayed in various museums throughout the world. The envelope system provided privacy to the writer and if the seal had not been broken, the recipient would know that no one else had read his mail.[16]

Papyrus: Another of the vegetable writing materials is papyrus. Apparently invented in Egypt where long papyrus stalks grew along the banks of the Nile River, especially in the Nile Delta region. This versatile plant was also used as a fuel, food, medicine, for clothing and for rope manufacture.[17]

The thick stalks were peeled off from their outer layer and then cut into flat strips. The strips were laid out on boards in a crisscross weaving pattern and gently beaten with a wooden hammer.

The result, after drying, was a very strong, flat writing surface that could be rolled up. Not only was it a versatile writing material, it was also very light.

Large sheets could be manufactured and after polishing each sheet with pumice stone, it was ready for the scribe. The longer the text of the message, the longer the papyrus page could be made. Papyri many meters long have been discovered.

The average length of a religious or business roll is about ten meters, although some are known to have been up to 40 meters long. [18]

For storage, they were rolled to form scrolls. For practical use, a long scroll was somewhat inconvenient. To be read, a scroll had to be unrolled with one hand while the other was busy re-rolling it simultaneously, causing a small portion to be seen at any one time. Because of this, scroll length became standardized.

Standard sizes meant that long works, such as Homer's *Iliad* and *Odyssey*, needed 24 scrolls to accommodate them, resulting in the division into 24 books. Similarly, the books of the Bible have been shaped by prescribed scroll sizes. Long books such as *Samuel and Kings* needed to be divided into two parts while short books like the *12 Minor Prophets* could be combined into one single scroll.[19]

Writing was achieved by using pen and ink. The pen was a slit reed and the ink was a mixture of lamp soot with gum and water. This combination was highly durable, as evidenced by the survival of thousands of fragments of written texts. The papyri itself was the weakness of the system. The ink had tremendous longevity but fire, dampness and insects easily destroyed the organic papyrus.

Pic Courtesy: Papyrus Roll-Data Storage Through the Years, Time, US, Issue dated: Sept.8/ Sept.15,2014, p-34.

Archaeologists have found documents written on papyrus, rolled up, tied with a string and sealed with a clay stamp on which the mark of the authority is impressed.[20]

Parchment: Parchment as a writing material was a surface made from animal skins. Writing on animal skins was known to be widespread in the Assyrian period. "The oldest known animal skin scroll is said to be that of the Egyptian 12th Dynasty."[21] Parchment is basically leather. Leather and parchment both begin by using the same treatment process, with the two just having a different ending. Skins were washed, soaked, cleaned of hair and residual flesh, and carefully smoothed out. To create leather, the skins were then treated with tannin. For parchment, the skins were not tanned but dressed with alum and dusted off with fine chalk. The thinner hides of goats and sheep were preferably used for parchment over the thicker hides of bulls. Young animals produced the finest parchment and this was often referred to as vellum.

The dating of the Hebrew manuscript on parchment found at Muraba'at, near the Dead Sea, was attested to 750 B CE "Parchment appears to have become the normal writing material from this time on for permanent records while administrative matters were still recorded on papyrus."[21]

Parchment was much more durable than papyrus and could withstand hard weather and usage. Papyrus rolls were easily torn or damaged by fire, and many had to be rewritten or copied.

Unlike papyrus, parchment had a reverse side that was not so suitable for writing. It was the hair or wool side that had been scrapped but could never be made as smooth or as white as the face side. For this reason, the good surface became the inner face of the roll and the outer was used only as decorative surface of a scroll.

Almost all ancient classical literature was written on parchment. However, the development of writing materials through ancient times is as fascinating as it is exhaustive. Millions of pieces of ancient communications have helped to record the past, and with hundreds of archaeological excavations ongoing, it is certain that millions more will be discovered and re-read.

Nobody knows the number of media that have been used for pictographs and writing, but we do know many survived the millennia. In Mesopotamia, the material of choice was clay – cheap, abundant and durable, but difficult to reuse. Mesopotamian scribes cut reeds from the marshes and pressed them into the clay, making the characteristic wedge-shaped marks of cuneiform.[22]

Ancient Egyptians wrote on ivory, bone, papyrus and leather, and linen, which they inked with ochre (natural earth pigment) and carbon. For ceremonial occasions, the ancient Egyptians carved stone on monuments. Today, an even more fragile material-bark may play an equivalent role in the understanding of early Buddhism. The Script of Indus valley civilization, one of the most advanced, has not been fully understood yet. Experts from all over the world are working on the problem. Scholars see a ray of hope in Mesopotamian language that is already known since people who lived in Mesopotamia had an active trading relationship with people living in the Indus and referred to them as "Meluhhans" in some Mesopotamian texts. Scholars and experts believe that for the possible existence of such a script, one has to look in Iraq or on the coast of Arabia, where trading between Mesopotamia and Indus valley civilization occurred.

Written on bark in the ancient language of Gandhāri, the language of ancient Gandhārā, they apparently contain the first known Buddhist texts.[23]

A chronological record of writing in the Indian subcontinent has been preserved in British Museum: Over time, people living in India have used many different writing systems. These systems were generally developed to record different types of information as the need arose.

The first Indian script, developed in the Indus Valley around 2600 BCE, is still undeciphered. Thus, it is not possible to fully understand this civilization as we have no readable records of their beliefs, history, rulers or literature.

Later Indian scripts like Brahmi and Kharosthi were developed to write both official and local languages. Great epics, royal inscriptions, religious texts and administrative documents were all written using these scripts.

Through these sources, we are able to learn about the literature, mythology, history and beliefs of ancient India.

Panini's book called the *Astadhyayi* was written in about the 4th century BCE It is a complete grammar of the Sanskrit language.

Sanskrit was a language only used by the literate elites. Panini's work helped to begin the standardization of the language. Scholars today are able to learn many things about what the language was like in Panini's time because he had written his book outlining so much about the structure of the language. An agreeable timeline could be:

2600 BCE	Early settlements develop into urban civilization.
1500 BCE	Oral composition of the Vedas
900 BCE	Oral composition of the Mahabharata
700 BCE	Oral compositions of the Upanishads
300 CE	Introduction of Sanskrit and Prakrit languages, Brahmi and Kharosthi scripts in use. Asoka converts to Buddhism
100 CE	Composition of the Bhagavad-Gita
600 CE	Translation of Buddhist texts into Chinese

The Vedic Civilization – far more ancient than the Greek – spread from India to Europe via Anatolia, Thrace, and Greece and from there to

Western Europe. The direction of flow was from India to Arabia and then to Europe. Evidence shows that Vedic tradition entered Europe sometime before the early 14th century BCE. The Rig Vedic tradition and its literature almost certainly came in to existence sometime long before the earliest civilization of Mesopotamia, Sumeria and Egypt.

The written Veda did not emerge until the Devnagri script was invented and that was during post Indus-Saraswati Civilization.[24]

According to Tibetan records, there were three great libraries in the University of Nalanda.[25]

"Indians made major contributions to a vast number of fields, especially mathematics, astronomy, metallurgy, alchemy, medicine and agriculture. India's water harvesting and management techniques are something we can still learn from. Metallurgical advancement, like the corrosion-resistant iron pillar in Delhi's Qutub complex, was other achievement. There were texts on sustainable agriculture, today we talk of organic farming but it was practiced widely in India in those days."

"Pre-modern mathematics has foundations in India. From 8th Century to 6th century CE *Shulabasutras* knew the Pythagoras theorem. Modern Arabic numerals originated in India. The decimal place-value numeral system evolved in India around the 3rd or 4th century CE Aryabhata conceived the earth as rotating sphere in space, which causes the apparent rising and setting of the sun. Varahamihira disagreed and Brahmagupta derided Aryabhata-but unlike medieval Europe, the intellectual climate in India was free and tolerant of dissent."

"Centuries ahead of Europe, Brahmagupta envisaged mathematical infinity and proposed that zero and infinity are mutually inverse notions. In fact, the concept of infinity underlies much of Indian science and technology. Many of those techniques of algebra and astronomy travelled to Persia and Arabia. Some went to medieval Europe. Overall, texts suggest the flow of mathematics was much more out of India than into it."[26]

Transmitting knowledge: In the ancient world, technological knowledge was disseminated through personal contact among traders who went out in search of metals and other commodities, and also by craftsmen through their work on metal, stone, leather, and the other mediums. These craftsmen passed their skills to others by direct instruction or by providing models that challenged other craftsmen to copy them. This transmission through intermediary contact was occurring between the ancient civilizations and their neighbors to the north and west during the 2nd millennium BCE[27] The pace quickened in the subsequent millennium, with distinct new civilizations arising in Crete and Mycenae in Troy and Carthage.* Finally, the introduction of the technique of working with iron profoundly changed the capabilities and resources of human societies and ushered in the classical civilizations of Greece and Rome.

China: Civilization flourished continuously in China from about 2000 BCE, when the first of the historical dynasties emerged. From the beginning, it was a civilization that valued technological skill in the form of hydraulic engineering for its survival. It depended on controlling the destructive floods of the Huang He (Yellow River). Other technologies appeared remarkably at an early date, including the casting of iron, the production of porcelain, and the manufacture of brass and paper. It simply amazes us today how marvelously quick they were in inventing paper, ink, types made of clay and printing. In 105 CE, Ts'ai Lun (50–121CE), a courtier in the imperial court, invented paper. Little did he realize that he was opening one of the most epoch-making chapters in the history of humanity. He refined and popularized the process of mixing tree fibers and wheat stalks with the bark of mulberry tree, then pounding them together and pouring the mixture on to a woven cloth to create a lightweight writing surface. These blended fibrous sheets

---

* *Carthase is near modern Tunis - destruction of Carthase represented decisive Roman Victory and end of Punia War. Troy is in modern Turkey (Truva in Turkish) - Homer first mentioned story of Troy in Iliad and Odyssey.*

were improvement over bamboo and wood, which were awkward and heavy, and silk, which was expensive.[28] The invention was a giant leap for mankind as, the paper later gave rise to currency, bureaucracy, and constitution.

Battle of Talas, 751 CE, was a military engagement between Arab Abbasid Caliphate and Chinese Tang Dynasty Among the prisoners of war captured by the Arab soldiers after the battle were a number of skilled Chinese artisans, including Tou Houan. Through these skilled workers, first, the Arab world and then the rest of Europe learned the art of paper-making. None of the combatants could have predicted that this battle would be instrumental in transmitting a key invention from China to the Western world: "the art of paper-making, a technology that would alter world history forever."[29]

(At that time, the Arabs controlled Spain and Portugal, as well as North Africa, the Middle East and large swaths of Central Asia.)

Soon, paper-making factories sprang up in Samarkand, Baghdad, Damascus, Cairo, Delhi and in 1120, the first European paper mill was established in Xativa, Spain (now called Valencia). From these Arab-dominated cities, the science and technology spread to Italy, Germany, and across Europe. In Europe, paper began a century's long battle for prominence with parchment until the invention of movable type in the fifteenth century that led to a steep rise in demand for the production of books that parchment could no longer satisfy. The eighteenth century saw paper made from linen and cotton rags that were replaced by wood and other vegetable pulp in the early nineteenth century. The Song Dynasty*

---

* *Yu the Great of Song dynasty was the most inventive and doggedly dedicated. He was first to discover how to tame the raging floods of Yangtze River and assist agriculture, catapulting mankind forward on the march of progress. There are estimated 600,000,000 acres of irrigated land worldwide today; all made possible by the efforts of Yu the Great. Yu's historical achievements won him a place in Chinese folklore and he is regarded as one of the three sage kings of China. (BBC Knowledge, October 2014, p-98 Chapter- In Focus)*

that ruled China from 960–1280 CE was one of the most innovative and technologically vibrant rulers. Keeping its best traditions, one of the alchemists in 1041 CE Bi-Shang shaped a series of reusable, moistened clay tablet, inscribed an individual character upon, it and fired them to harden and make them permanent and in the process invented movable type.

Printers use to take these characters and lay them within an iron frame coated with a mix of resin, turpentine, wax and paper ash, arranging the characters to reflect that was to become a printed page. Bi-Sheng failed to be recognized for his invention, like Johannes Gutenberg, until several years after his death. Unlike Latin-based western alphabet that required much fewer letters, Bi-Sheng worked in a language with over 5000 distinct characters, many of these required several pieces of types to complete and all of them required to be made in multiple numbers These copies were wrapped in paper, ordered according to the first syllable of the pronunciation and stored within the wooden-framed cases, when not in use. Bi-Sheng contribution was recorded by the Chinese scientist Shen Kuo in the series *Dream Essays* in which he says, "Bi Sheng movable types – for printing hundreds of thousands of copies, it was marvelously quick."

The multiplicity of Chinese characters and symbols was one reason for the failure of Bi-Sheng's invention to impact significantly upon Chinese society, in contrast to Gutenberg's process in fifteenth-century Europe. The other problem was the clay tablets itself was manifestly unsuitable for large-scale printing and was not at all durable. A similar situation arose in Korea, where metal typesetting was invented. The English language, miniscule by comparison in alphabet, was the perfect candidate for movable type.[30]

There have been sporadic instances in the history of inventions and discoveries that for various reasons, credits elude the actual inventor or discoverer. Bi Sheng of Song dynasty in China, actually, was the first to conceive the movable type, created about 5000 characters in clay to satisfy the complex Chinese language and fired it to give a concrete shape. This was almost 400 years before the famous German goldsmith Johannes Gutenberg created his movable types in metal.

The links between China and the West remained shaky until modern times, but the occasional encounter such as that resulting from the journey of Marco Polo in 1271–95 alerted the West to the superiority of Chinese technology, and stimulated a vigorous westward transfer of techniques. Western knowledge of silk working, the magnetic compass, paper-making, and porcelain were all derived from China.[31]

Early in the 17th century the natural philosopher Francis Bacon recognized three great technological innovations: the magnetic compass, the printing press, and gunpowder as the distinguishing achievements of modern man, and he advocated experimental science and technology as a means of enlarging man's dominion over nature. The present study will discuss in detail one of the epoch-making inventions: the printing press.

Mass Media in the Beginning: It wasn't that the world lived in a resigned manner before printing became possible. Information has always remained a cardinal thrust of mankind, and today we are simply amazed at the amount of labour and aesthetics that were put in to prepare information and to disseminate them, even without printing.

Prior to the invention of printing press, information used to be disseminated by word of mouth, exchange of private documents or the pasting of notices in public places. Since ancient times, one of the most popular methods of disseminating orders of the public authority has been by beating of drum in streets, haats, bazaars, etc. The rock and pillar inscriptions of monarchs also disseminated through royal orders and directives. Of course, there wasn't any direct method to collect public feedback or reaction, but it wasn't that feedbacks were not important. Public feedback and reaction were important as of today, but due to absence of any direct method, it was done indirectly as we shall see as the journey progresses. Gutenberg's printing press gave an escape velocity to information dissemination, which effortlessly transferred the world into an Age of Information.

Journalism in India is closely linked to the evolving phases of democratic form of governance, which in itself is a legacy of the British parliamentary system.

The conflict between the Crown and the people in England since early 17th century till the firm establishment of constitutional monarchy after the Glorious Revolution of 1688 provided grounds for rapid development of journalism in England, and by early 18th century, it took firm roots there. In contemporary India, however, the divine right of kings continued to find its echo in the oft-quoted adage*: Personifying the Emperor of Delhi as representative of God himself.

Thus, in the absence of conflict between the rulers and the ruled, the ground was not conducive in this country for growth of journalism. Initially Indian psyche, and for that matter anywhere in the world, have shown infinite patience to tolerate the worst type of tyrannies and there have been rare occasions when they have arisen against it. As a matter of tradition, administration was left entirely in the hands of kings, and complete confidence was reposed in him. The king was paid revenue and in return, people expected protection from him for their life and property.

In fact, people in general never really participated in the administration of their country before it became independent in 1947. Not surprisingly, literature and philosophy of that period reflected this psyche. Kalidasa (c.4th century AD) has also thrown light on the character of kingship.

---

* दिल्लीश्वरो वा जगदीश्वरो वाः *Ruler of Delhi is like God, Hindu scriptures also have held the same view:* बालोअपि नावमन्तव्यो मनुष्य इति भूमिपः, महती देवता राजा नर रूपेण तिष्ठति (मनुस्मृति अध्याय 7, श्लोक 8))*Even if king is a child he should not be disobeyed, King is a supreme God who (is here) in the form a human being (to discharge his duties), #* प्रवर्ततां प्रकृतिहिताय पार्थिवः/सरस्वती श्रुतिमहती न हीयताम् (अभिज्ञान शकुंतले सप्तमाङ्के भारतवाक्यम)

He says, "While the king should engage himself in administration leading to the welfare of his subjects, people should concentrate on cultivating learning (based on Vedas)."

Kautilya has also dwelt at length on the necessity of a secret organization for the State to collect news (Intel) regarding the enemies of the State, foreigners and unsocial elements. However, this type of intelligence – though collected carefully and methodically from day-to-day working – was exclusively for State purposes and was not open to public. It was thus quite distinct from journalism, which is open to all.

Even during 14th century India, news-writers and their role in administration and method of collecting information have been cited in Ibn Battuta's *Travelogue of India.*

According to Moroccan Muslim traveller and explorer Ibn Battuta* (1304–1369), it seems, there was an effective system of communication in place when he came to visit India in 14th. century. There were two modes of sending mail from one point to another. One was to carry it by horses arranged by the State and other was to carry it by men designated for the work. These were people who carried messages written by news-writers of the Emperor's court from one place to another, and from there to the final destination. A series of men were involved in the process.

"After every one third of a Kosa (about 2 miles or 3.2 kms) there was concentration of population taking shape of a village. Every such village was provided with a Dak Chowky (Post). Each Chowky was manned by a Herkara. (Type of postman/communication post). Every Herkara was provided a two-yard stick with ghungroos (anklet bells) atop it. Sound of ghunghroos from one Herkara of preceding post alerted the herkara of the next. Without wasting any time the next herkara would take the message

* *Represented and reproduced on the basis of Ibn Battuta ki Bharat Yatra ya Choudahvin Sadi Ka Bharat by Madan Gopal PP 1-2 – National Book Trust 2005 (4th reprint) First edition published by Shrikashi Vidyapeeth Varanasi, 1993.*

forward. [It was much like a modern relay race in which messages took the place of baton]. To avoid delay, Herkaras (perhaps) completed the distance by running all through. Another way of carrying messages was through horses. Though one would in general tend to believe that distribution through horses would have been faster, but not according to Ibn Battuta, he says that distribution of mail by men weren't only faster and easier but in way were much more credible. Apart from messages, be it dry fruits from Khurashan (a province in north-west Iran now) or any other precious things were sent to the king by this mode. Not only that, hard core criminals after being averted in any corner of the empire were sent to the Emperor's Court by this mode. Ibn Battuta gives another example when water of holy Ganges was sent for Emperor's use through this mode to Daulatabad. The distance from Ganges to Daulatabad was covered on foot in forty days."

"News writers in the Emperor's Court not only recorded the arrival and departure of every traveller to the kingdom but documented every aspect of the traveller as well, i.e., his appearance, his dress, way of living, number of dasas (servants) he had, and number of horses he carried with him. All possible details of every traveller were documented, leaving almost nothing to chance or guess."

Under Akbar (1556–1605), news was collected on the largest possible scale, not only throughout the empire, but also at the court where every action, howsoever small it might be was recorded, checked and forwarded to the official concerned and preserved for record. In 1557, Akbar established a record office which helped later historians to gather materials for chronicle. The record office used to have a copyist on its staff that wrote abridged versions of documents, and presented them to the *Vaque-a-Nevis* or the news-writer of the court. The circulation of manuscript/newspaper was extant during Aurangzeb's rule (1659–1707) when soldier were supplied with such newspapers.

Tulsidasa has also characterized the popular view of indifference towards administration.* But whatever the form of Government, a ruler cannot be indifferent to public opinion. Therefore, some system to collect people's reactions to administration is vital for the safety of the State and accordingly, it has to keep itself informed of both in respect of the views of foreign states as well as its own internal matters. Thus, rulers in India – as indeed elsewhere – from ancient times have maintained organizations to collect intelligence to enable them not only to frame their state policy but to also ensure survival and expansion.

"Traditional empires and civilizations simply did not have the communication technology required to hold it together beyond a certain point of expansion, and when they split into conflict and instability, they left behind in each region a relatively small, classically educated elite group of rulers and teachers who continued the classical tradition of learning and helped develop regional, vernacular culture among a much more numerous uneducated populace."

At the beginning of the 17th century, a functionary known as news writer, who had not thus far practiced as an independent profession but was generally a retainer at the court of some noble man, is credited with the laying of the foundation of profession of journalism in Europe. In India, too, it was a custom of emperors to appoint such news writers or *Vaque-a-Nevis* in each district, and these writers were charged with the responsibility of sending reports of important events of the locality, and these documents used to be the foundation of Government policies.[1] But such reports were often badly distorted as an independent contemporary observer has pointed out.

Dr. Francois Bernier, a French physician, who served at the Courts of Shah Jehan and Aurangzeb during the years 1656–1668, writes:

---

* *कोउ नृप होहिं हमैं का हानि (It hardly makes any difference to (me) whoever is going to be the king)- रामचरितमानस, अयोध्याकांड, कैकेयी-मंथरा संवाद*

> *"The provincial governors are so many petty tyrants, possessing a boundless authority and as there is no one to whom the oppressed subject may appeal, he cannot hope for redress, let his injuries be ever so grievous and ever so frequently repeated. It is true that the Great Mogul sends a Vaque-a-Nevis (a newswriter) to the various provinces; that is, persons whose business it is to communicate every event that takes place, but there is generally a disgraceful collusion between these officers and the governor, so that their presence seldom restrains the tyranny exercised over the unhappy people."*[2]

The following account is given by Venetian traveller Niccola Manucci, who lived at the court of Aurangzeb for some years:

> *"It is a fixed rule of the Moguls that the Vaque-a-Nevis and the Cofe-a-navis or the public and secret news-writer of the empire, must once a week prepare a sort of gazette or mercury, containing the events of importance. These news letters are commonly read in the King's presence by women of the mahal at about nine o'clock in the evening, so that by this means he knows what is going on in his kingdom. There are, in addition, spies who are also obliged to send in reports weekly about other important businesses, chiefly what the princes are doing, and the duty they perform through written statements. The King sits up till midnight, and is unceasingly occupied with the above sort of business."*[*3]

John Fryer, also a doctor, who served in India during 1672–681, has said that the failure of Aurangzeb in the Deccan was partly due to the false reports sent by his news-writers.[4] We find another reference to

* *According to H Baveridge's review in the Journal of Royal Asiatic Society, October, 1908, in 1828 Colonel James Tod sent some hundreds of original manuscripts and newspapers of the Moghul Court (1660) to the Royal Asiatic Society in London.*

the corruptibility of news-writers about the middle of the 19th century in the memoirs of Major-General Sir William Sleeman (Rambles and Recollection of an Indian Official). Referring to the Kingdom of Oudh and the defeat of a certain Ghulam Hussain, he says:-

> *"Ghulam Hussein was so ashamed of the drubbing he got that he bribed all news-writers within twenty miles of the place to say nothing about it in their reports to Court, and he never made a report of it himself."* [5]

In another context William Sleeman says that the King of Oudh employed 660 newswriters and that they were paid on an average between four and five rupees per month. Commenting on their low remuneration he says, low pay was one of the reasons that easily made them vulnerable. [66]

The following extract from the work of S.C Sanyal throws more light on the state of journalism in early 17 th and 18 th century:

The earliest distinct mention of ante-typographic newspapers is to be found in the *Muntakhabat –al Lubab* of Khafi Khan where we find the death news of Raja Ram, of the House of Sivaji, brought to the Imperial Camp by the newspaper. The great historian also gives us clarity to understand that the common soldiers in Aurangzeb's time were supplied with newspapers. Aurangzeb allowed great liberty to the press in the matter of news. As an example, he cites a case of a Bengal newspaper commenting rather severely on the matter of the Emperor's relation with his grandson Mirza Azim Oshan. In *Seir-ul-Mutaqherin* there is a mention made of Kaem Khan, son of Jafer Khan, head of the Post and Gazette Office. During the declining period of the Mogul Empire, the manuscript press continued their circulation. Thus, we find popular historians noticing that in the summer of 1792, the public newspapers of Delhi stated that the Emperor had expressed to Mahadji Sindhia and the Peshwa his hope that they would enable him to recover the imperial tribute from the Bengal Provinces – "I wish to mention two famous men who were connected with journalism in the 18th century. One was Asaf

Jah's minister, Azim-ul-Omrah. He was originally a gentleman of the press but rose in time to be Prime Minister. The other was Mirza Ali Beg the Imperial Gazetteer (*vaqu-a-negaur*), the doyen of journalists throughout the empire. This officer was in constant attendance upon His Majesty. In his time the official intelligencer in Guzerat was Abdul Jaleel, a Syed or Belgram, who was also paymaster of the forces in that important province."[7]

In first half of the eighteenth century, the East India Company frequently availed services of the news-writers to acquaint the Indian courts of matters of intelligence. A case in instance is that of one Ramchandra, a Vakil, who was sent on March 27, 1704 to Hugli and was to write down in his own language with the following direction: "He is to declare to the Governor, the *Buxie* and *Vaque-a-Nevis* that we have appointed him vaqueel in Hugli for the affairs of the English"*.[8] Thus a news-writer found an altogether new role for him.

Gutenberg's remarkable machine and thereafter: Printing is a process of reproducing text and illustration on paper (or any other medium suitable for printing) by applying ink under pressure. Science and technology involved in printing of newspapers has accelerated the composition of texts or illustrations and technologies were used to develop paper that could withstand high speed of printing and development of ink-types that were highly durable. The earliest form of press incorporated a wooden block with raised letters on one side. Such blocks were arranged in frames and inked so that when pressed on to paper an impression of letters was produced. Unfortunately, the blocks disintegrated with use and so could not produce many copies. It was a bit time consuming for craftsmen to produce new blocks for letters and illustrations.

---

* *In contemporary times some Indian journalists have been assigned to ambassadorial posts. This was the point, perhaps, from where the concept of Public Relations and Corporate Communication started taking shape that has now grown in to a full-fledged profession and is a branch of journalism and mass communication combined.*

The first permanently recorded news that we know about was carved on stone and set up in prominent places in Babylonia, the Assyrian city. In general, such carved stone carried news from the battlefield. The Roman Empire, which covered most of Europe, made it necessary for news and instruction to be carried back and forth and from the entire length and breadth of the empire.[1] Romans were known for their good road building skills that facilitated to a great extent in faster delivery of news from and to the empire headquarters in Rome. Thus, the first newsletter called *Acta Diurna* or *Daily Doings* (the distant ancestor of our newspaper) was born. This was in Julius Caesar's time. When most of the Roman Empire finally fell in the fifth century CE, Europe split in to small, warring states. For six centuries no one recorded or carried the Daily Doings. Grass grew between the beautifully laid stones of the great Roman Roads; the mountainside no longer echoed to the thunder of horses' hooves. The art of reading and writing withered away in Europe, except in the Churches where it was kept alive by monks and priests who copied out religious books by hand.[2] 800 years later, in 713, the Chinese Tang Dynasty published the *Kaiyuan Za Bao*, a news bulletin handwritten on silk.[3]

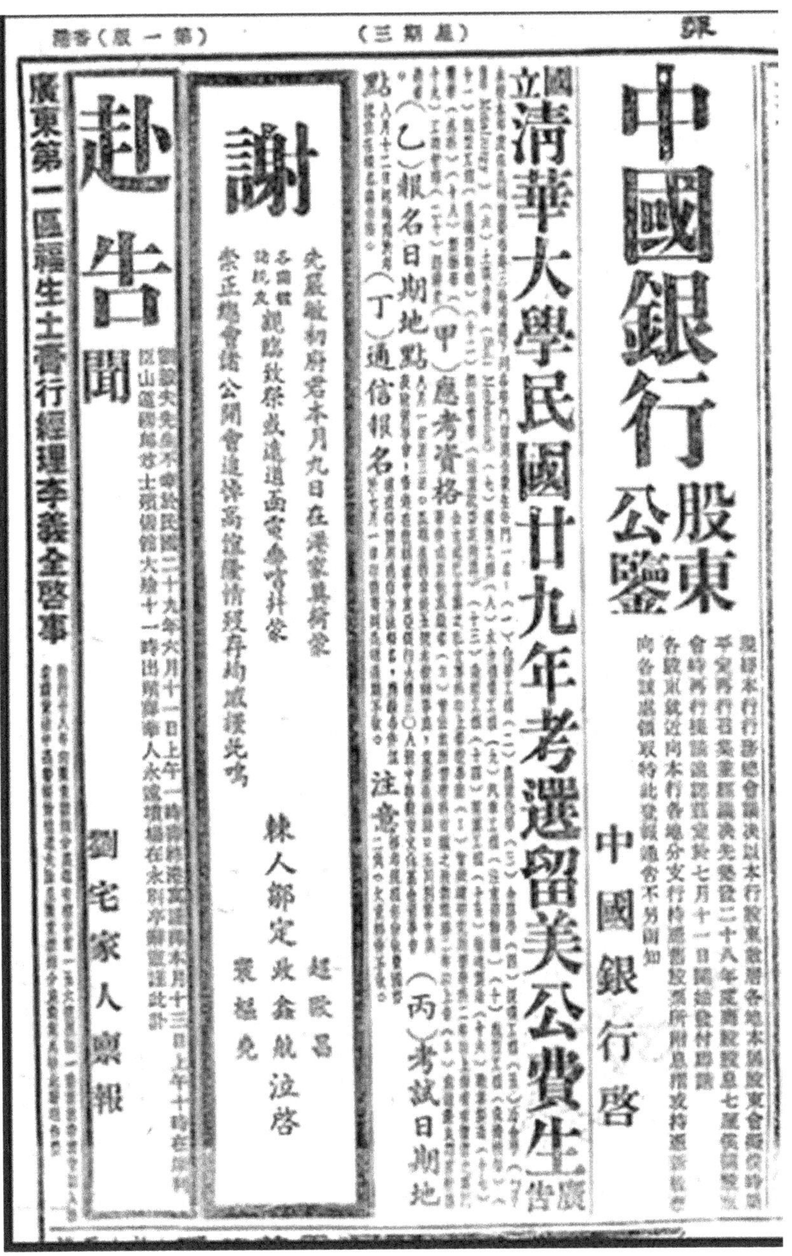

中國銀行股東公鑒

中國銀行啓

國立清華大學民國廿九年考選留美公費生廣告

(甲)應考資格

(乙)報名日期地點

(丙)考試日期地

(丁)通信報名

注意

謝

棘人鄒定永鑫航泣啓

訃告

聞

廣東第一區福生土膏行經理李義全啓事

劉宅家人稟報

A Chinese newspaper Kaiyuan Za Bao (Bulletin of the court) published during the Tang Dynasty between 713-734. Photo credit: Twitter a/c of HYPERLINK mailto: Freedy.me@Freedynews, it was hand written on silk

At the start of the 15th Century, every text had to be laboriously written by hand. Another copy of the same work required same labor and effort to be put in. Naturally, the process had its limitation. The mass production of work was not possible. In spite of the limitation, we are simply amazed by the quantity and quality of manuscripts that were so laboriously prepared.

Johannes Gutenberg (circa 1400–1468), an oft-unsuccessful German businessman, recognized the moneymaking potential of mass- produced books and set about experimenting with printing methods. Using the typesetting technologies of Asia, a modified recipe of oil- based ink and a design built on the olive and grape screw-type presses used by farmers across Europe, Gutenberg developed his famous printing press. The most important and original contribution was Gutenberg's letter moulds, which he concocted from a metal alloy and which were highly durable.[4] The new system was simple, still tedious, but much more efficient than anything that had ever existed before. Each page of text was made up of individual letters arranged in a type tray. The process could take a full day of work, but that type tray was reused over and over again to produce multiple copies of a page and then it would be re-set for other pages without wasting the metal letters, making mass production feasible for the first time. None of these features existed in Chinese or Korean printing or in the existing European technique of stamping of letters on various surfaces or in woodblock printing. Gutenberg's invention remained the source of basic elements of typesetting for 500 years. Gutenberg's first large- scale printing – a set of 200 illustrated Latin Bibles – rolled off the press in 1455. Every copy had been pre-sold before he'd even set the last page

Word spread quickly from Germany across the continent about Gutenberg's remarkable machine.[5] Though the man himself died poor in 1468, losing his savings in a legal battle against a business partner, his system became a commercial success.[6]

The printing revolution that began with Johannes Gutenberg laid the ground work for the expanded role of methods of dissemination of news by its introduction of the means to provide mass circulation of print media or in modern terms – the newspaper – for the first time. And today, Johannes Gutenberg is one of the most celebrated inventors in history, mainly because his *chef d'oeuvre*– the printing press – allowed his story, as well as the stories of thousands of others, to be set down on paper.[7]

It is clear, however, that his invention drew heavily upon previous experiences with block printing – using a single block to print a design or picture, and on developments in typecasting and ink making. It also put heavy demands on the paper industry, which had been established in Europe since the 12th century, but had developed slowly until the invention of printing press and the subsequent vogue for the printed word. The printers found an enormous demand for their product, and hence, the technique spread rapidly and the printed word became an essential medium of political, social, religious, and scientific communication as well as a convenient means for the dissemination of news and information. By 1500, almost 40,000 recorded editions of books had been printed in 14 European countries, with Germany and Italy accounting for two-thirds, ranging from classical Greek texts to Columbus' account of the New World.[8] Few single inventions have had such far-reaching consequences. Initially writing, and later on printing, was an important step in the advancement of civilizations, but few books were produced and they reached a limited number of people. These books were mostly religious, copied by clerks and clergy. It was only when the printing press was developed that the knowledge and ideas were spread more widely.

Gutenberg's printing press spread literature to the masses for the first time in an efficient and durable way, shoving Europe headlong into the original Information Age – the Renaissance. Gutenberg's medieval machine was so capable that it remained virtually unchanged until the 19th century and the advent of steam-powered presses.[9] The invention of movable type has been likened to the birth of the internet. It was the technological breakthrough that powered the dissemination of ideas during the Renaissance and the humanist explosion of learning in early 16th century.[10] Gutenberg was a master of many trades as he was his own typographer. He was also the publisher who undertook to risk capital in the selection and preparation of material to be printed for sale; he was presumably the man who designed the layout of each page; he may have done whatever editing was required, and he certainly either printed or supervised as an assistant in the printing of the finished product. In the course of years, many of the functions at first performed by one man came to be divided among several.[11]

[*]The development of the movable type printing press and its rapid spread to numerous European cities made many things possible, affected nearly all aspects of life, and changed literate society forever in a way that deserves scrutiny even today. Its impact was so vast as to make it largely immensurable, according to many historians.[12] This had led many interested in European civilization to dismiss the printing press and its impact rather quickly, or, at best to give it a quick nod of acknowledgement and move on to developments and characteristics easier to gauge.[13] The invention of printing represents a watershed event in the world history, between print culture and scribe culture, and catalyzed the Italian Renaissance, the Protestant Reformation and the

* *Johannes Gutenberg, Courtesy: "Die großen Deutschen im Bilde" (1936) by Michael Schönitzer, Page URL:https://commons.wikimedia.org/wiki/File:Johannes_Gutenberg.jpg,File URL: https://upload.wikimedia.org/wikipedia/commons/d/d7/Johannes_ Gutenberg.jpg. de Larmessin, Public domain, via Wikimedia Commons.*

Scientific Revolution.[14] This is although the widely accepted view but not the only one. Some consider that it was an extension of the scribe culture and "the dawn of printing did not really mean end of an era and commencement of another; it was a gradual transition from one medium to another."[15] Others, however, acknowledged the tremendous impact of printing had on every aspect of European life and culture. Printing ensured knowledge transfer on a much larger scale from elite and private domain to public domain. This beauty of the technological innovation broadened the base of knowledge in the society that opened the door for hectic activities in many spheres of social life. Scribe culture was important; it was this culture that provided a firm base from where giant strides in many directions were taken. The Martin Luther protest is a case in point. Luther's protest against indulgence in *Ninety-Five Theses* (1517) had been unwelcome. Many Catholics sympathized with the view that Salvation could be earned only by penitence rather than buying remission of sin. Luther's disputation with Erick (Representative of Pope and Professor of theosophy with whom Luther debated the issue) helped crystallize his ideas, especially that salvation was a matter of faith alone. The Pope was convinced that Luther was a threat and in June 1520, issued a bulletin of excommunication. And the Reformation had begun.[16] Luther, though excommunicated, lived to see most of North Europe abandon Rome for new Protestant Churches.[17] Many tempt to consider it as beginning of a new era[18] that was made possible only by the printing press of Gutenberg on which many copies of *Theses* were printed and distributed among people.

Literacy levels, still low among the general population in Europe, crept upwards as the cost of books steadily dropped and book fairs became yearly occurrences in most major cities during the early years of the Renaissance. The printing press was one of the key factors in the explosion of the Renaissance movement, historians say.[19] Access to standard works of science and technology especially stimulated and spread new ideas quicker than ever.

Thus, throughout Europe, pamphlets and chap book led to great national newspapers of succeeding centuries, particularly in Europe's great metropolitan centers, which ultimately provided a medium for the dissemination of news of historical events such as wars, resolutions and governmental affairs as well as the means of social and cultural communication both within nations and linguistic groups, and across nations.

There seems to be more than one opinion about the first newspaper after the advent of printing press. Some consider *Notizie Scritte*[20] from the great trading city of Venice to be the first newspaper as we know it today. *Notizie Scritte* meant "Written Notices", and were first posted in streets where anyone who could read was allowed to see it on payment of a small coin called a Gazetta, which led to news sheets being nicknamed Gazettes, the word that for many years remained associated with names of newspapers. However, there is a larger agreement that in 1605, Johann Carolus (1575–1634) published the first printed issue of *Relation aller Fürnemmen und gedenckwürdigen Historien.* (*Relation* in short) in Strasbourg, France, thereby giving the world its first newspaper. Initially, Corolus copied his newsletter by hand and sold them to rich subscribers. But in order to make his publication affordable to more people, and thus increase his revenue, he bought a printing shop in 1604. Despite his modern approach, *Relation* did not survive. Hence, today the Dutch daily *Haarlems Dagblad* (after merging with the *Oprechte Haarlemsche Courant* from 1656) is the world's oldest existing paper.

Haarlems Dagblad

Oprechte Haerlemse Courant 1656

Paolo Giordano wilde nu roman met een climax

Dode potvis op Razende Bol kapitaal waard

FC Barcelona speelt gelijk tegen Paris St. Germain

Fietsersbond wil Rode Loper naar noord doortrekken

Protest tegen sluiting van gevangenis in Haarlem in 2016

Personeel van Koepel komt in actie

Fietser klem onder truck op hoek Spaarndamseweg

Twijfels over alarmsysteem bij wapenroof

Proefkrant op compact formaat

VANDAAG

Uitbijlage met een schaartje

Haarlems Dagblad: Est. 1656, a local tabloid in Netherlands, though went through acquisition and merger, Considered to be the oldest continuously published newspaper in the world. Photo credit: one of the latest issue available on the net, https://www.haarlemsdagblad.nl/?utm_source=search.yahoo.com&utm_medium=referral&utm_content=/

Initially the medium was viewed skeptically by some. Benjamin Harris found out as much when he tried to establish the United States' first newspaper *Publick Occurrences, Both Forreign and Domestick* in 1690. The paper was meant to be "furnished once a month (or if any glut of occurrences happen oftener)." But he was forced to abandon his plan after only one issue of *Publick Occurrences* when outraged government officials decided that his publication contained reflection of a very high order and had been printed "without the least Privity or Countenance of Authority."[21]

The Gutenberg press was a crude one in comparison to its later versions, but it gave the long-awaited momentum to printing. On the sidelines, improvement in quality of newsprint and ink-types continued. In 1884, Benjamin C. Tilghman invented Sulphite process, where wood is heated in liquor containing an excess of Sulphur dioxide to create pulp. Later, in 1884 German inventor Carl. F. Dahl found that using caustic soda and sodium sulphate in a "white liquor" resulted in a much stronger pulp. This pulp produced pages that was named Kraft, after German word meaning "strength".[22] It also had recoverability more than the sulphite process so the chemicals could be recovered for future use, making it more efficient. It overtook the sulphite process as the dominant form of pulping and is still used today. More reliable ink- types were developed using powdered minerals, plant extracts, berry juice and pigments.[23]

The names that ring down the years from 1800s onwards are those of engineers, builders and inventors. Watt, Stephenson, Faraday, McAdam, Edison, Bell, Morse, Marconi...every one of these inventors influenced the growth of newspaper industry, directly or indirectly. The great innovations in communications technology, however, were derived from electricity. The first was the electric telegraph, invented or at least made into a practical proposition for use, on the developing British railway system by two British inventors Sir William Cooke and Sir Charles

Wheatstone who collaborated on the work and took out a joint patent in 1837. Almost simultaneously, the American inventor Samuel F.B. Morse devised the signaling code that was subsequently adopted all over the world. In the next quarter of a century, the continents of the world were linked telegraphically by transoceanic cables, and the main political and commercial centers were brought into instantaneous communication. The first transoceanic cable was laid across the floor of Atlantic from Field Foihomomerum Bay, Valentine Island in Western Ireland to Heart's content in Newfoundland. The first communication occurred on August 16, 1858, reducing the communication time between North America and Europe from ten days the time it took to deliver a message by ship to an instant.

The electric telegraph was followed by the telephone, invented by Alexander Graham Bell in 1876, and adopted quickly for short-range oral communication in the cities of America and at a somewhat more leisurely pace in those of Europe. About the same time, theoretical work on the electromagnetic properties of light and other radiation was beginning to produce astonishing experimental results, and the possibilities of wireless telegraphy began to be explored. By the end of the 19th century, Guglielmo Marconi had transmitted messages over many miles in Britain and was preparing the apparatus with which he made the first transatlantic radio communication on December 12, 1901. The world was thus being drawn inexorably into a closer community by the spread of instantaneous communication. These altogether paved the way for teleprinters, which formed an integral part of newspapers offices around the world. Their particular sound became synonymous with newsrooms of newspapers establishments.

In India, Hindi newspapers initially depended on news-feeds from English teleprinters only till late 1977–1978. *Hindustan Samachar* and *Samachar Bharati* started feeding the news from their Hindi teleprinters network in this period but their use was limited. During the 1980s,

Hindi and other vernacular journalists started going abroad for coverage of international events. They used to file their copies in Roman that was later transcribed in Hindi and other languages by the editorial staff. *UNI* and *PTI* started their Hindi news service *Varta* and *Bhasha* much later.

Elizabeth Grey in her book *The Story of Journalism* had shared an anecdote regarding the use of this electric telegraphy and how it changed the world that we live in forever:

The first news of its kind to hit the headlines in England came only a few months after the system had been introduced into the country and a nineteen-mile (30.4 kms) length of telegraph wire set up by the Great western Railway, from Paddington station to Slough.

During the morning of January 6, 1845, the operator at Paddington Station, still a little nervous of this new magic was startled to receive the following message:

"A murder has just been committed at Salt Hill and the suspect was seen to take a first-class ticket for London by train which left Slough 7.42 AM, he is in the garb of hawker with a brown overcoat which reaches nearly down to his feet – he is in the last compartment of first- class carriage."

"Was it a joke? The operator dared not risk it. Pausing only a moment to get his breath back, he hurried out of his office and down to street of nearest police station.

"It was no joke and police took it seriously, too. When 7.42 AM train to Slough arrived at Paddington Station, plain-clothed policemen arrested the suspect from the first-class carriage. Not surprisingly, his trial caused a sensation, and he was eventually executed for the murder."

And John Tawell, the convict, was the first casualty of this electric current. The handy deliverables which a telegraphist used to jot down to a conclusive meaning came to be popularly known as telegrams.

Between the 19th and 20th centuries the telegram was such an icon for speeding up deliveries of message that it also formed an integral part of intense storytelling and was aptly immortalized by character artist Kanhaiya Lal in the Hindi feature film *Khandan* (starring Sunil Dutt and Nutan, directed by A Bhimsingh in 1965).

Radio was another invention which further speeded up the delivery of news. There are many stories attached with radio messaging, as cited above. Certainly, these inventions were not merely sensation mongers. They altogether gave the news a fresh perspective. It was clear that in time to come, definition of news would depend more on science and technology than any other factor contributing to it.

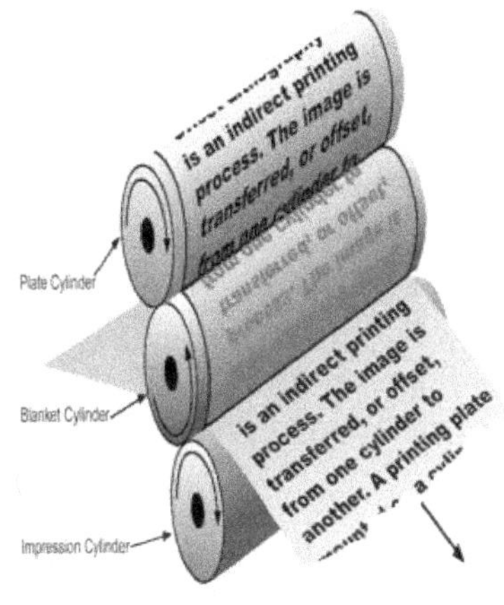

In England, a journey towards faster production of newspapers could begin only at the turn of the 19th century. It was still very slow to be produced and was expensive as well. To succeed as mass-circulated newspapers, it had to come out of the clutches of 250 sheets an hour, and this was first realized by John Walter II (his father John Walter was founder of *The Times*, London). He saw that unless something was done to make printing both faster and easier, no further progress of any kind could be made. He decided that steam power – already being used in textile industry – could, and should be harnessed for printing as well.[24]

Fredrich Koeing, a German, actually invented the steam-power printing press, but it was John Walter who first installed it secretly in the printing shop of *The Times* in November 1814 (secretly because the hand printers may fear that increased automation would threaten their livelihood). But once installed, it was soon accepted. In addition, Koeing invented a simplified method of inking types – another time and labor saver, which also made possible technically the use of larger sheets of paper and to increase the page size of newspapers.

From 250 impressions an hour, output grew to 1000 to 2000. Later, the larger and more complicated machines developed by the Englishmen, Applegraph and Cooper, were able to turn out as many as 8000 sheets an hour. This was done by locking the chases of type in segments around a central horizontal cylinder so that the movement became rotary (round and round) instead of reciprocating (backwards and forwards), and by incorporating an ingenious arrangement of feeding points at different levels which enabled first four, and then eight operatives to feed the machine at the same time.[25] Rotary was another landmark arrival for newspapers in 1846. It came at a time when it was most needed.[26] This invention by Richard March Hoe (1812–1866) took the concept of mass media to a yet higher scale. With the rotary movement that revolutionized the printing press, came stereotyping – the biggest change in actual construction of the printing machine since its invention. Now instead of type being set flat, it was molded onto a curved plate filled on to a continuously revolving horizontal drum. *The Philadelphia Public Ledger* in the US was the first newspaper to use the rotary in 1847.[27] This was the year John Walter III – who succeeded his famous father and was still not satisfied with the speed at which newspapers were being produced – realized that no further progress in printing could take place while machine themselves were dependent on the speed at which men could feed them. This problem was solved when a paper strong enough to be fed into the machine in a continuous strip from a giant roll was developed in America. In 1866, a machine which came to be known as the Walter press was designed and built for *The Times.*

The reel or web-fed machine led the paper between two sets of stereo-printing cylinders – the first printed four pages simultaneously as one side, the second printed the reverse side. Each printing cylinders had its own set of ink rollers. A cutter separated the continuous sets in the sheets carrying eight pages. The sheets then went up to the distributor, on which "two takers-off" were employed – alternate sheets falling to either side. Manned by only three men, the Walter Press could produce 12,000 eight pages complete newspaper in an hour. With some attention and refinement, it remained as a basic ultimate machine, while the quality of newsprint kept on improving so that it could withstand maximum speed (and paper was not torn in between printing).

Printing and photography- Another important process that was to make a vital contribution to modern printing was discovered and developed in the 19th century – photography. The first photograph was taken in 1826 or 1827 by the French physicist J.N. Niepce using a pewter plate coated with a form of bitumen that hardened on exposure. His partner L J M Daguerre and the Englishman W.H. Fox Talbot adopted silver compounds to give light sensitivity, and the technique developed rapidly in the middle decades of the century. By 1890s George Eastman in the United States was manufacturing cameras and celluloid photographic film for a popular market, and the first experiments with the cinema were beginning to attract attention.

Between 1830 and 1855, the Mercantile Community of Calcutta had contributed towards the maintenance of a system of semaphoric communication which had been organized by the Government for the service of the capital.[28] But this system was not that effective in foggy weather or in the night. This system continued till the advent of the electric telegraph.[28]

In between 1840–1850 carriages drawn by horses or bullocks were in use. In 1850s India saw the opening of railways and along with them, electric telegraph – both inland and transoceanic – made its appearance. However, the cost of transmission of news through electric telegraph was high, and therefore, the press availed this facility on a limited scale. In 1869 the Suez Canal was opened, and this revolutionized communication between Britain and India by drastically cutting the period of voyage.[29]

Pressure on manual composing was quantitatively eased by the arrival of linotype and monotype composing machines. This transition from manual to mechanical composing formed an integral part of printing press in India in the period from 1960s to 1970s, but were limited to big publication houses. A linotype unit used to be a huge machine with typewriter like keys, where compositor was able to type and the result was received in a line. Hot zinc metal was used as a basic material (that's why hot metal printing) on which every letter of composed line appeared on the raised surface on the thin zinc plate. Inking the raised surface and use of pressure thereafter resulted in print. An option of bold type face became available after some time wherein one could get some texts in bold faces. Today, this may seem quite a drudgery to go in to the detail of a such a huge machine which worked as typewriter for press, but these were the machines which made the publication of daily newspapers a reality. As it always composed a line in single column width, a little mistake required the composed line to be replaced with a fresh one. Hence, editors were required to put in the highest degree of accuracy while writing the news copies. On the other hand, compositors and proofreaders were also required to put in the same degree of efficiency. An army of editors, proofreaders and compositors – apart from workers on printing press – were required to put in their collective effort in three-shift duties to produce a single edition of newspapers. Newspapers in 1970s and 1980s worked so precisely that they were almost error- free and became a hallmark for improving language-skill and keeping oneself updated with happenings from around the world. Still, it had its own limitation. Linotype or monotype machine could only be used for texts. For headline of bigger font size, press had to depend on manual composing. A newspaper printing press was a mixture of hand and machine composing till 1980s in India. After 1960s newspaper printing presses in India were using rotary on a big scale for printing. Capital cities like Patna, Bhopal (and Indore too), Lucknow (Varanasi, Kanpur), Hyderabad, Trivandrum catered to sizeable circulation, apart from Calcutta, Madras, Bombay and Delhi.

Newspaper technology was slow to arrive in India. The technological changes that have been described above took almost a century to reach India. Through 1970s and up to the 1980s big Indian newspaper houses had stereotype printing machines that could finish work in three shifts (morning, afternoon and night) to produce newspapers. News copies were mostly hand written or written on type writers. Increase in literacy pressed the demand further. In the 1960s and 1970s, the Indian press was undergoing revolutionary changes so far as acquiring newspaper technology was concerned. *The Statesman* was first to use steam power for newspaper production. *The Times of India*, Mumbai and Delhi were successfully producing world-class products. To suit its facsimile copy system, *The Hindu* in several of its satellite plants had taken to web-offset. *The Indian Express* had set up a high-speed web-offset press at Bombay. *The Hindu* was using photo type setting in Madras Chennai). But these were few houses that were capable of introducing new newspaper technologies.

According to the Registrar of Newspapers for India, the number of newspapers (for which circulation data was available for the year 1979) was 635. The total circulation of these was placed at 13.03 million. Size of the circulation of newspapers varied widely. Nearly half of the newspapers brought out less than 5,000 copies each; on the other hand, there were newspapers with circulation of more than 50,000 copies each. Of the 325 newspaper presses taken into consideration, 31 had letter-press printing and hand-composing facility, 158 mechanical composing, 70 hand-printing presses and 104 had plate and block- making facilities. It required a huge amount of manpower in both editorial as well as production. Costs involved in arranging manpower and machine and other necessities kept the big newspapers confined to metros. Small newspapers still did their work with hand-fed machines, and they catered to a small circulation.

In the period cited above, in hand-composing, about 29 lakh type cases were estimated to be in use in India. The average weight of a type case ranges from 20 kg for English to 33 kg for some regional languages. The total weight of metal in type cases with printing presses in India was estimated to be about 70,000 tones. The newspaper presses had an average of 103 type cases while the average for Government presses was 362.6 type cases.[30] Newspaper technology had been progressing and changing so fast that modern newspapers plants became unrecognizable from what they looked like a couple of years ago. Although it was in the area of composing that there had been revolutionary changes, it led to consequential changes in related processes and procedures as well.

In the West, electronics invaded the text composition process in a big way. The changes had not been confined to speed, efficiency and versatility. The entire environment in the composition room had radically changed. There was no longer the dirt, noise and the high amount of lead fumes – a health hazard. Compositors could now work in air-conditioned comfort in a silent and clean atmosphere.[32]

It was further advancement in science and technology that helped editorial manpower to speed up their output, cut cost further, and only then did it become conducive for big newspaper houses to make inroads into state capital cities. Entry of big houses in places other than capital cities changed the whole social dynamics and turned many barren lands in to thriving newspaper business grounds.

In 1798 it took nearly 2 months for the news of Nelson's victory of the Nile[*] to reach London. 103 years later, in 1901 radio signals were carrying messages across thousands of kilometers in a split second, and the news they carried was being set up on linotype machines printed on steam-driven rotary process, automatically fed by continuous reel of

---

* *The Battle of Nile remains one of Royal Navy's most famous victories, and has remained prominent in popular British imagination, sustained by its depiction in a large number of paintings, poems and plays. One of the best-known poems about the battle is Casabianca, which was written by Felicia Dorothea Hemans in 1826 that describes a fictional account of the death of Captain Casabianca's son on the French ship Orient.*

papers and carried across the length and breadth of the country by the fast railway services. It was the greatest explosion of industrial progress the world had ever known.

And the pattern for the future was set: new technologies facilitated (and made economically feasible) massive print-runs, journalism targeted itself to vast readership, advertising became more and more crucial for the financial support of the press, ownership vested with very rich individuals or joint stock companies; readership patterns hardened along lives of social class and competition became increasingly desperate.

Role of the Media in the National Movement Leading to Independence

2

Although the East India Company had installed a printing machine in Bombay in 1674 and another in Madras in 1772, the first newspaper that made its appearance on the Indian scene was *Hicky's Gazette*. It was *Hicky's Gazette* that laid the foundation stone of journalistic endeavors in India. For various reasons the journey of *Hicky's Gazette* was not a smooth one. The situation Hicky faced, the manner in which Hicky fought for the freedom of the press was the foundation stone on which architects of Indian Independence movement, including journalists and politicians, built a solid structure. The seeds of dissent were sown. The British East India Company was so averse to the idea of newspapers in India that it had already frustrated an attempt by one William Bolts, a merchant of Dutch Extraction.

In 1766, one William Bolts*, affixed the following notice to the door of the Council House in Calcutta and other public places:-

"To the Public:

Mr. Bolts takes this method of informing the public that absence of a printing press in this city is of great disadvantage in business and making it extremely difficult to communicate such intelligence to the community

---

* *While in London, in 1772, William Bolts published a book Consideration of Indian Affairs Particularly Respecting the Present State of Bengal severely criticizing British Affairs of his time.*

that is of the utmost importance to every British subject. He is ready to give the best encouragement to any person/s who are versed in the business of printing, to manage press, the types and utensils of which he can produce. In the meantime, he begs leave to inform the public that having in manuscript many things to communicate, which most intimately concern every individual, any person who may be induced by curiosity or other more laudable motives, will be permitted at Mr. Bolts's house to read or take copies of the same. A person will give due attendance at the hours from ten to twelve any morning."

And on April 18, 1767, it was recorded:

> *"That Mr. Bolts having on this and many other occasions endeavored to utter an odium upon the administration and to promote faction and discontent in the settlement, has rendered himself unworthy of any further indulgence from the Company and of the Company's protection. That therefore he be directed to quit Bengal and proceed to Madras on the first ship that was to sail from that Presidency in the month of July next in order to take his passage from thence to Europe in September."*[1]

Thus, William Bolts, whose disputes with the Court of Directors were protracted, was deprived of carrying out his intention to publish a newspaper. Governments all over the world had primarily shown reluctance to newspapers, but finally they gave in. After Bolts' efforts were finally aborted in 1767, it took thirteen long years when *Hicky's Gazette* finally arrived on the Indian scene. We can only imagine the resistance a newspaper publisher had to face in that period. Was the journey that Hicky embarked on an easy one? We can see it in Hicky's meteoric rise and mercurial fall. Barring few exceptions, the future editors were determined to take the Government head on, and a journey towards independence had begun. This journey took a quantum leap after the First War of Independence in 1857.

But first, Hicky's story and stories of several steps taken by the Government to gag the press.

Hicky's Meteoric Rise and Mercurial Fall: The pioneer of the Indian press – James Augustus Hicky – was also on the forefront of leading the fight for freedom of the press. Hicky was a dedicated journalist of a high reputation and his uncompromising spirit remains a lighthouse of inspiration even today. Hicky is credited with bringing out the first newspaper of the country. Researchers working on Hicky has termed his paper to be the first newspaper in Asia. His newspaper *Hicky's Bengal Gazette or the Original Calcutta General Advertiser*[2] (Referred to as *Hicky's Gazette* in the text for ease of reading and as it was popularly came to be known) was published from Calcutta (now Kolkata) on January 29, 1780. The newspaper carried his personal imprint to such an extent that it came to be popularly known as Hicky's *Gazette.* As for this venture, he said, "I have no particular passion for printing of newspapers, I have no propensity, I was not bred to slavish life of hard work, yet I take pleasure in enslaving my body in order to purchase freedom for mind and soul."[3] Hicky described his journal as, "A weekly political and commercial paper open to all parties, but influenced by none."[4]

Hicky's satirical pieces of personal nature were to a great extent popular among its readers, but it created ripples among the ruling class. Hicky's initial enthusiasm and his uncompromising nature in the long run invited a catastrophe in which not only the genius newsman's future was eclipsed but it was also a serious setback in the development of journalism in the country. His story of meteoric rise and mercurial fall establishes that freedom of press comes at a huge price.

HICKY's
BENGAL GAZETTE;
OR THE ORIGINAL
Calcutta General Advertiser.

A Weekly Political and Commercial Paper, Open to all Parties, but influenced by None.

59 From Saturday March 3d to Saturday March 10th 1781. No. VII

http://digi.ub.uni-heidelberg.de/diglit/hbg1781_7/0001

N Kumar Editor, editor of Bihar District Gazetteers, had indicated that an incomplete file of Hicky's Gazette was available at British Museum newspaper Library at Colindale and National Library in Calcutta. However, latest check indicates that British Museum newspapers Library at Colindale has been closed and majority of printed material is under embargo and has been moved to British museum site. Masts of few Indian newspapers are preserved and Hicky's Gazette is one of them. National Library at Calcutta does have a collection of the newspaper file under rare collections and is available @nationallibray.gov.in/nat_lib_stat_rare_others-html#anchor270721.Hicky's Gazette is best preserved at University of Heidelberg, Germany's website ***http://digi.ub.uni-heidelberg.de/diglit/hbg1781_1782_50/0001*** *and one can view a complete look of the great paper. (The Pic. above, Courtesy, University of Heidelberg)*

The administration strongly disliked its stance as open to all and influenced by none, and on November 14, 1780, the same year, it was served with the following order by Governor–General, and *Hicky's Gazette* was prevented from circulation through channels of General Post Office.[5]

14th November, 1780

Public notice is hereby given that a weekly newspaper called the *Bengal Gazette* or *Calcutta General Advertiser* printed by J.A. Hicky, has lately been found to contain several improper paragraphs tending to vilify private characters and to disturb the peace of settlement. It is no longer permitted to be circulated through channel of General Post Office.[6]

Hicky bitterly complained to the Governor-General's action and characterized it as the "strongest proof of arbitrary power and influence that can be given".[7] Incidentally the event marked the beginning of the struggle between a free press and the Bengal Authority.

Initial punitive measures made Hicky more hostile. He became more abusive and bitterly attacked Warren Hastings and Sir Elijah Impey. Impey (13 June 1732–1 October 1809) was a British judge, the first Chief Justice of the Supreme Court of Judicature at Fort William in Bengal.

In defense of his publication, Hicky wrote:

Mr. Hicky considers the liberty of the press, to be essential to very existence of English men. The subject should have full liberty to declare his principles and opinions, and every act which tends to coerce that liberty is tyrannical and injurious to the COMMUNITY.

A commendable statement indeed, but fate had something else stored for Hicky. Although a healthy press for a healthy rule has been advocated to be essential, but throughout the entire history of humanity – with sporadic exceptions – powers-that-be have hardly given ample scope and space for its media criticism, and the Bengal Government and *Hicky's Gazette* were no exception. So, in June of 1781, an armed band, including several Europeans, some sepoys and between three to four hundred peons, went to arrest Hicky under an order from the Chief Justice, acting under the Governor-General's instructions. He met force with force, and on refusing to be taken away, undertook to attend the judge in the court on being shown a legal authority for his arrest. But the court had been adjourned before he arrived and he was imprisoned until the next morning when he appeared before the Supreme Court to answer two indictments lodged by Warren Hastings. Hicky was slapped with ₹ 80,000/- bail (a huge amount in those days and beyond the payment capacity of Hicky), and accordingly remanded in jail for not paying the amount.[8]

Hicky's imprisonment did not mean extinction of his paper, for he continued to edit the *Gazette* from the prison and even maintained the same tone. In January1982, when Warren Hastings returned to Calcutta after his tour of North-Western provinces for some months, the case against Hicky was heard and he was sentenced with one-year jail term with a fine of ₹ 2,000/-.

In March 1782, Hicky published the following statement:

Mr. Hicky addresses his citizens and fellow subjects with heartfelt joy, and tells them that on March 7, 1782, the King's judges inclined to admit him to plead in *forma pauperis* in defending four fresh actions brought against him, this time by Warren Hastings, Esq., and that Mr. Counsellor Davis (for Plaintiff) did make a motion and plea in the bar of Mr. Hicky's types being exempted from seizure, setting forth that the said printing(metal) types did form a great part of Mr. Hicky's property and hoped their Lordship would protect the said types from being seized upon should judgement be obtained against him. This motion, the honourable King's judges strongly opposed as repugnant to the British Legislature and Constitution and treated it with contempt it so very justly merited. Thus, by protecting the types, they had protected the liberty of the subject and the liberty of the press.

Encouraged by this success, Hicky continued to assert that he was being unjustly persecuted by the Governor-General and the Chief Justice.

In this context, the opinion of one William Hickey, a contemporary attorney practicing in Calcutta, is of particular interest:

The (real) fact was that this turbulent man having published various paragraphs in his famous newspaper reflecting in the strongest and most abusive language upon both the public and private conduct of the Governor-general, Mr. Hastings, that gentleman at last resolved to make an example of author of such gross and indecent scandal by prosecuting him on the Crown and Criminal side of the Court for libels...... He (Hicky) was blessed by nature with considerable talent, but quite uneducated, violent in temper, especially when opposed or thwarted in any of his wild plans, to the highest degree.[10]

However, Hicky possessed doggedness and a persistence in the face of all calamities, which speaks well for the trader-printer turned journalist. A comparison of his brief career as a newspaperman with that of John Wilkes (the journalist who was on the forefront of fight for freedom of the press in Britain) is perhaps inevitable.[11] John Wilkes was one of the most intriguing and influential journalists; witty, fearless but also extravagant. Wilkes was several times elected to the British Parliament, but each time he was expelled and outlawed for his outspokenness and outrageous behavior. On one occasion, in his journal *The North Briton*, he accused the King of England of telling lies in his speech from the throne. Each time Wilkes was thrown out from the Parliament, he returned more powerful and more popular than ever.[12] In 1771, he was made Lord Mayor of London, and he used his position of authority to protect and fight for rights of newspaper reporters. One of his greatest victories was when he obtained permission for the press to print parliamentary reports.[13]

Despite criticism, Hicky certainly deserves to be remembered as the pioneer of the Anglo–Indian press. In spite of his best efforts, Hicky could not get his bill passed by the East India Company for printing its regulations. He addressed a representation to Secretary Hay, in which *inter alia* he said:

> *"From the well-known good things of your heart, it would be needless to say any more to you on the subject of getting my business done as quickly as possible, than to inform you that I am at present moment confined to my room and in the utmost distress with a family of helpless children."*[14]

His two subsequent reminders – also to Edward Hay – remained unanswered. After a good deal of effort on his part, he succeeded in getting his bill of ₹ 35,092/- passed for ₹ 6,711 /- only on condition of giving a full acquittal of all the demands to the Government. Hicky wished to be informed by what calculation or rule, the Board had made out so trifling a sum as they thought proper to allow him for the printing and paper of their military regulations. He addressed a memorial to the then Governor-General, Sir John Shore, praying for the payment of his bill in full, but in vain. Ultimately, straightened circumstances, financial stringency and utter helplessness compelled him to accept the amount of ₹ 6711.[15]

The unfortunate printer-journalist had waited sixteen years only to have his claims whittled down to a fraction of his demands. At the end, circumstances moderated Hicky's independence as a journalist and compelled him to seek favor from Warren Hastings, whom he had given offence on so many occasions in the past, and asked for his influence to get him appointed a deputy to the Clerk of the Calcutta Market,[16] a post which carried some monetary allowance so that he could support his family. Hicky dared much and lost much but his name has survived in the annals of Indian journalism.[17] The entire Hicky episode presents a vivid picture of how a press could be so arbitrarily silenced and how units of governance were in collusion with one another to deny what was rightfully due to him. In his case, justice was not only delayed but also denied. There are different opinions about the last days of Hicky in India. Some reference indicates that he died in a boat destined for China, it is surprising that Encyclopedia Britannica does not say a word about this Irish journalist.

Marques Wellesley (Governor-General of Bengal between 1798 and 1805, and later served as Foreign Secretary in the British Cabinet and as Lord Lieutenant of Ireland) took the extreme step of silencing the press and issuing guidelines that proved as the last knell in the coffin of free expression. Observations and remedial measures undertaken by him were not only archaic in nature but were also detrimental to the growth of a robust press in India.[18] His successors had a tough time in correcting his wrong doings. Further course of events suggests that the Government was not only keen at silencing the voice of dissent but also prompted other printer-publishers to come out, speak the voice of consent and get the official patronage. Entry of new newspapers after *Hicky's Gazzette* suggest that by silencing *Hicky's Gazette,* the Government was able to send a strong message for such future endeavors. Newspapers started competing with each other in getting favours from the Government rather than doing actual journalism.

Close on the heels of *Hicky's Gazette,* a second journal *India Gazette* appeared in November, 1780. Two businessmen, who sponsored the new journal, approached the Government with the following letter:

"To

The Hon'ble Warren Hastings, Esqr.,

Governor-General;

and

The Council at Fort William Calcutta.

October 4, 1780

Hon'ble Sir and Sirs,

Understanding that our plan of an intended publication of a newspaper has met with the favour of your approbation, we are encouraged to take the liberty of requesting the additional one of your further patronage; by granting us permission to send it to our different subscribers, out of Calcutta; by the Dawk, free of Postage; on our paying annually to the Post-Master-General such a certain sum as you shall think proper to direct; we likewise engage that no other article or writing whatsoever shall go under the said cover with the newspaper, or newspapers, and that each cover shall be endorsed *India Gazette*; as well as sealed with our joint names in Persian or indeed complying with any regulations you may be pleased to order. We also humbly beg leave to take, this opportunity of soliciting the favour of our being appointed Printers to the Hon'ble Company, at Calcutta; which should you think proper to confer, it shall be our stride and endeavour to do our duty; by executing with correctness and dispatch, all orders sent to our care.

We have the honour to be with the greatest

Respect, Hon'ble: Sir and Sirs,

Your most obedient and humble servants,

B.Messink.,

Peter Reed."[19]

It appears that the authorities were on the lookout for some newspapers which could toe their line and also counteract the so-called evil influence of *Hicky's Gazette*. The *India Gazette* fulfilled this role. Within the next few years, the following journals also emerged from Calcutta: -

i. *Calcutta Gazette* (February, 1784 under Government patronage) *ii.* *Bengal Journal* (February, 1785)

iii. *Oriental Magazine* or *Calcutta Amusement* (April, 1785)

iv. *Calcutta Chronicle* (January, 1786).

All these papers looked to the Government for patronage and concessions of various kinds. The *Bengal Journal* wrote to the Supreme Council proposing postal concessions and also suggested that it would print any Government advertisement, which the Board might think proper to order, free of charge.[20] These newspapers generally concentrated on the news of England and devoted scant attention to the news of the country.

One William Duane, a native of North America and of Irish ancestry, had arrived in Bengal in 1787 as a private citizen in the service of the East India Company. After a short spell of service under the Company, he became editor of the *Bengal Journal.* In the course of the Maratha War, which Governor-General Lord Cornwallis was conducting personally, a rumour spread in Calcutta that the Governor-General, i.e., Cornwallis had died, and Duane published it in his paper, adding that it had been attributed to a certain Frenchman. (Lord Cornwallis was the first Governor-General under the new Act; He held office between 1786 and 1793, representing the British Government and was answerable to the Board of Control).

Reference to a certain Frenchman irked Col. De Canaple, who was styled the Commandment of the Affairs of the French Nation in India. He wrote to the Bengal Government for satisfaction. The news turned out to be wrong. Cornwallis was not willing to grant toleration to any person who might help create unnecessary friction with the French or other powers. So, in consultation with the Law Officers, he ordered the arrest and deportation of Duane. However, the journalist escaped deportation on the intervention of a French agent who informed the Government that (unfortunately, in the meantime) complainant Colonel de Canaple had actually died and Duane may kindly be excused. But Duane* came in conflict with the authorities soon again. Sir John Shore was determined to deport him. Duane asked for time to settle up his affairs before being sent to England. But he was refused any further stay in India and was deported to England. No compensation for his property stated to be worth ₹ 30,000 was paid for.[21]

Explaining his action in a private letter to Rt. John. Henry Dundas, on 31 December 1794, Sir John Shore wrote:

> *"Our newspapers in Calcutta have, of late, assumed licentiousness too dangerous to be permitted in this country. I have ordered one of the editors to be sent back to Europe. His name is William Duane, and I think, you will agree with me, that his conduct did not entitle him to the protection of the Company."*[22]

The Supreme Court of Judicature upheld the Government order, and thus set the precedent for expulsion of foreign journalists from India for press offences. The contemporary newspapers were mostly concerned with military matters. The East India Company was, however, fighting with all its resources for supremacy in India and thus, naturally regarded any public discussion on military affairs as highly objectionable and dangerous to their interest. In between 1791 and 1798, many editors were reprimanded for discussing military subjects.

Mr. Hosley, editor of the *Calcutta Gazette*, was censored. However, he asked for pardon and on promising to refrain from such publication in future, and was excused.[23]

One of the criticisms against the contemporary journalists is that they frequently resorted to attacks on the private character of individuals and sometimes criticized the official measure without sufficient

* *Later on, Duane went to America and began to edit Aurora which was known for extreme anti-British policy. Perhaps the bitter experience of Duane at the hands of the British in India may have been responsible for his attitude towards them.*

information.[24] In reply, it may be said that the Government had the handy weapon to deport the editors and proprietors of newspapers who came for adverse notice and the Supreme Court had also approved such action. This should have generally been regarded as sufficient to hold the foreign journalists always *in terrorium*. Even then the Marques of Wellesley, who was governing the country at that time, took a hard line and declared, "I am resolved to encounter the task of effecting a thorough reform in private manners here, without which the time is not distant when the Europeans settled at Calcutta will control the Government if they do not overturn it. My temper and character are now perfectly understood and while I remain, no man will venture *miscere vocem* who has, not made up his mind to grapple instantly with the whole force of Government."[25]

Wellesley issued the following declaration on May 13, 1799 for the control and guidance of the proprietors of the newspapers published in Calcutta:

1. Every printer of a newspaper to print his name at the bottom of the paper.
2. E Every editor and proprietor of a paper to deliver in his name and place of abode to the Secretary to the Government.
3. No paper to be published on a Sunday.
4. No paper to be published at all, until it shall have been previously inspected by the Secretary to the Government, or by a person authorized by him for that purpose.
5. The penalty for offending against any of the above regulation to be immediate embarkation for Europe.

The following rules were formulated for the guidance of the Secretary who was to act as Censor and prevent:

1. The publication of all observations on the state of the public credit, or the revenues, or the finances of the Company.

2. All observations respecting the embarkation of Troops, Stores or Specie or respecting any Naval or Military preparations whatsoever.
3. All intelligence respecting the destination of any ship, or the expectation of any, whether belonging to the company or to individual.
4. All observations with respect to the conduct of Government or any of its officers, Civil or Military, Marine, Commercial, or Judicial.
5. All private scandal or libels on individuals.
6. All statements with regard to the probability of war or peace between the Company and any of the Native Powers.
7. All observations tending to convey information to any enemy, or to excite alarm or commotion within the Company's Territories.
8. The re-publication of such passages from the European newspapers as may tend to affect the influence and credit of the British Power with the Native States.

These regulations and restrictions rigidly curtailed much of the independence of newspapers. In view of these stringent measures, the proprietors and editors of newspapers had no choice but to submit to the Government, lest they chose to close down their papers. But there is no denying the fact that the journalistic world viewed the Government action with dismay and unhappiness.[26]

In 1801, Wellesley had come to the conclusion that the establishment of an official gazette would be the best method of silencing the existing press which he felt was "evil of the first magnitude…useless to literature and to the public, dubiously profitable to the speculators, (they were) only to maintain in needy indolence, unfit for any subsistence." (But the scheme was ultimately abandoned on grounds of cost involved)

The authorities were always on the lookout to find faults with the press and were not prepared to tolerate the slightest delay on their part.

The journals could not publish any military news, except such as may be sent for communication under the signature of one of the Secretaries of Government. They had also to submit the proof of their journals for approval. This usually delayed the publication of papers and meant loss of subscribers who could not allow much indulgence to them.

Lord Minto's successor, Lord Moira (afterwards Lord Hastings) enforced new rules for the control of printing press on October 16, 1813. These rules were set out in the following letters addressed to the proprietors of the *India Gazette, Telegraph, Mirror, Calcutta, Gazette, Hurkaru, Star* and *Hindostanee* presses, and one Mr. De Souza:

Gentlemen,

The rules established for the control of the printing offices at Calcutta having undergone revision by Government, I am directed to acquaint you that the Right Hon'ble the Governor-General in Council is pleased to desire your observance of the following rules:

First- That the proof sheets of all newspaper including the supplements and all extra publications be previously sent to the Chief Secretary for his revision.

Secondly- That all notices, handbills and other ephemeral publications be in like manner previously transmitted to the Chief Secretary for his revision.

Thirdly- That the titles of all original works proposed to be published be also sent to the Chief Secretary for his information who will thereupon either sanction the publication or require the work itself for his inspection, as may appear proper.

You will of course consider the rules established on the 13th May, 1799 and 6th August, 1801 to be in full force and effect, except in so far as the operation of them may be modified by the foregoing instructions.

I am and ca,

G. Dowdeswell.

The other person of note was James Silk Buckingham, a former mariner with the Company. The life and time of Buckingham re-affirms that administration at that time was in no mood to allow freedom of the press of any degree to publishers of newspapers. Buckingham, right from the beginning, practiced responsible journalism, refrained from personal attacks or character assassination of any short and laid the foundation of one of the most popular newspaper the *Calcutta Journal*, a bi-weekly.[27]

On October 2, 1818, the *Calcutta Journal* appeared as bi-weekly at a rupee a copy. By profession James Silk Buckingham was a mariner, but his success as editor of *Calcutta Journal* was remarkable. He declared in his journal that he conceived his duty "to admonish Governors of their duties, to warn them furiously of their faults, and to tell disagreeable truths." In the absence of any legislature, he considered the press to be a necessary check on any irresponsible government, in other words – the Government would be subject to public scrutiny.[28] He injected long-awaited freshness in selection of news, made it broad based and the attention was drawn to prevailing grievances as the inefficient state of the police. At the same time, he created open space for public correspondence where grievances were ventilated. This paper was described well conducted, "independent and clever" and drew a good response from readers which constituted mainly civil servants, military officers and merchants. In 1822 its subscriber's base was more than 1000. At that time, value of the enterprise was estimated at £40,000 of which Buckingham himself owned three-fourth and his annual income was £8000.[29]

Buckingham was critical of trade monopoly given to the East India Company and advocated that competition should be opened to whoever was willing to risk his health and fortune. Naturally, the East India Company was not happy with what Buckingham was doing, but his popularity of fair and acceptable journalism prevented them from cracking in directly. First, *Calcutta Journal* was countered by another journal *John Bull in the East,* published by the Company's employees. But it was not for long that coercive tactics were used to bring *Calcutta Journal* under the Company's influence. Before authorities revoked the license of *Calcutta Journal* and passed the order of Buckingham's deportation, he very bravely asserted, "It is the freedom of the press which is the object of their hatred and scorn. While power of banishment without trial existed, no English man could hope to enjoy independence of mind in the performance of his public duties or the promulgation of his opinion in India."[30]

This was followed by usual rituals like appointing a select committee to examine the claims of compensation to Buckingham and recommending that he ought to be paid (but amount to be decided by the Company) and finally refusal to pay anything by the Company. Buckingham's friends, all of whom stood for the freedom of the press, brought a bill for Buckingham's compensation in British Parliament which was carried by a vote of 48 to 13. Thereupon, Buckingham's opponent rallied and the motion for a second reading was defeated by 185 to 81.[31] Thereafter, Buckingham's friend opened a public subscription to provide an annuity for him and his wife. Lord William Bentinck (Lord William Bentick was the first Governor-General of British-occupied India. Everyone else before him was the Governor of Bengal, Fort William]), who in the meantime had retired from the Governor-General post, chaired the meeting of the subscription committee. He publicly expressed the view that there was a general feeling in Calcutta that Buckingham had been unjustly treated. He had built up a journal from a small beginning to become the most widely circulated newspaper in India. The appeal succeeded in purchasing an annuity of £100 for Buckingham and £80 for his wife. However, in 1851, when Buckingham was 65, he was granted a civil list pension of £200, but he lived for only four years to enjoy the grant.[32]

Calcutta Journal continued even after Buckingham's departure under the editorship of Mr. Sandys, who having born in India, could not be deported. He was assisted by two Britishers, Sandfor Arnot and James Sutherland. These two gentlemen were to have the right to veto the publication of any matter that might be considered detrimental to any class of the society.

The fight for the freedom of the press which began in 1780, continued till 1834 when Buckingham was finally deported to Britain. The period also saw the emergence of Lord Bentinck and Sir Charles Metcalfe (1785–1846, acting Governor-General of India from March 1835 to March 1836. Born on 30 January 1785 in Kolkata, educated at Bromley and Eton, he came back to Calcutta in 1801 at the age of sixteen as a writer in the Company's service) who, as Governor- General, tried his best to provide an ambience in which Indian press could breathe more easily. Whereas Bentinck adopted a policy of non- intervention, Charles Metcalfe went ahead in passing the Act XI of 1835 which repealed the 1823 Press Regulation in Bengal (and also the Bombay Press Regulation of 1825 and 1827). Lord Bentinck intervened only once in the wake of the first Burmese War when on account of reduction of their allowances, army officers showed great discontentment against the administration, and therefore, Lord Bentinck decided that press should be kept under rigid control so that there may not be any mutiny in the army.[33] Otherwise, he did all to encourage the prosperity of the press between 1831 and 1833, as is apparent from the numerous editions of Calcutta newspapers. Sir Charles Metcalfe believed in free expression of all classes of people. But, this freedom brought about by this duo survived for barely two decades.

Outside Bengal Presidency, *Madras Gazette* first faced censorship in 1795. It was required to submit all general orders of Government for scrutiny by the Military Secretary before publication. Free postage facilities were withdrawn, and it was decided to impose the levy at the delivery end. Bombay's first newspaper, the *Bombay Herald,* came into existence in 1789. The *Courier,* which was published a year later, carried advertisements in Gujarati. The *Bombay* Gazette was published in 1791, and the *Bombay Herald* was merged into it the following year, being officially recognized for purposes of official notifications and advertisements in the same terms as the *Madras Courier*.[34]

First, the Santhal uprising of 1855-1856 and then the Sepoy Mutiny of 1857 came as a real shocker to British rule in India. With its entire arsenal in place and continuous exercises to curb the press, it could not get even a little trace about the storm that was brewing throughout the country. Naturally, it shook the confidence of the Raj in its channels of communication and futility of its steps taken to curb the press. This resulted in yet other steps to curb the press.

As a consequence to the Great Revolt of 1857, a new Act (Act XV of 1857) was promulgated on June 13, 1857 to regulate the establishment of printing presses in India. This infamous Act was known as the "Gagging Act". This was to be operative for one year.

Some of the provisions of this "Gagging Act" were:

A license from the Governor-General of India in Council or the Executive Government of the Presidency was to be a prerequisite to opening a printing press. If anyone opened a press in contravention of this rule he was to be liable for conviction before a magistrate to a fine not exceeding ₹ 5,000 /-or to imprisonment not exceeding two years or both.

An unlicensed press was liable to be seized altogether with the books and papers found on the premises of the printing press.

a. Copies of all books and other papers printed at a press licensedunder the Act were to be immediately forwarded to the Magistrate or to such other person granting the licence.

b. Government might prohibit the publication of any particular newspaper, book or other printed paper within the territoryof its jurisdiction or not. A contravention of this rule was toattract, on conviction before a Magistrate, a fine not exceeding ₹ 5,000 or imprisonment not exceeding two years or both and every such book or paper was to be seized and forfeited.

c. Under the provisions of this Act, the *Bengal Hurkaru* was suspended from September 19 to 24, 1857 and a fresh license was granted to it when the offending editor (Sidney Laman Blanchard) tendered his resignation. The printers and publishers of Indian journals such as *Doorbeen*, *Sultan- ul-Akhbar* and *Samachar Sudhavarshan* were prosecuted for publishing articles being seditious and they were committed for trial. [35]

Vernacular Press Act of 1878: As if the gagging was not enough, Vernacular Press Act IX of 1878 was enacted to curtail the freedom of the Indian-language (i.e., non-English) press. The Act was proposed by Lord Lytton, (Edward Robert Lytton Bulwer-Lytton or Lord Lytton was the first Earl of Lytton and was a nominee of the conservative Government of Benjamin Disraeli, who was entrusted with the charge of the Governor of Bengal at a very crucial time). then Viceroy of India, and was intended to prevent the vernacular press from expressing criticism of British policies, notably the opposition that had grown with the outset of the Second Anglo-Afghan War (1878–80). The Act excluded English-language publications. It elicited strong and sustained protests from a wide spectrum of the Indian populace.[36]

It was designed to prevent seditious appeal to the people. It required printers and publishers of any paper in an Indian language to enter into a bond to not publish anything likely to incite feelings of disaffection against the Government or antipathy between persons of different races, caste and religion in India. If a newspaper contravened this regulation, it was first to be warned of the offence and if repeated, the press was liable to be seized. A censorship was framed by the Government for those who wished to avoid such a risk.

The law was repealed in 1881 by Lytton's successor as viceroy Lord Ripon (Lord Ripon, originally known as George Frederick Samuel

Robinson, was the Governor-General and Viceroy of India from 1880 to 1884.). On December 7, 1881 a bill was introduced for the repeal of this Act on the grounds that in the opinion of the Government, circumstances no longer justified the existence of the Act. However, the resentment it produced among Indians became one of the catalysts that fueled India's growing independence movement. Among the Act's most vocal critics was the Indian Association (founded 1876), which was generally considered to be one of the precursors of the Indian National Congress (founded in 1885). Lord Ripon's repeal of Lytton's Vernacular Press Act in 1881 coincided with the abolition of the Press Commissionership. The relaxation in the attempted exercise of political control by the British over the press in India opened the way for vigorous debate on the future of India. The writings of the Indian intelligentsia found their way into an increasing number of new newspapers, both Anglo-Indian and vernacular.[37] His successor Lord Dufferin (one of the most successful diplomats of his time. His long career in public service began as a commissioner to Syria in 1860, where his skillful diplomacy maintained British interests while preventing France from instituting a client state in Lebanon.) adopted an attitude of friendliness towards the Indian press. He also permitted Government servants to contribute for the press for the first time. His refusal to sanction prosecution against the *Amrita Bazar Patrika*[*] on the report of his agent, Sir Lepel Griffin, in Central India on the alleged ground of libel may be cited as an instance of his liberal policy towards the indigenous press.[38] Thus, the Government not only started opening up towards the press but it also frustrated attempts to take Indian press to task by authorities on minor offences.

---

* *The Amrita Bazar Patrika disclosure of confidential foreign office documents concerning Kashmir led to the passing of the Act. Its object was to prevent disclosure of official secrets. The authority to release adverts and newsprints was already with the Government. But Hindi press not only never lost its patriotic tone but never shied away from its responsibility towards the society and nation.*

The historical events that followed provided space for the Indian press to come together and express their opinion. Apart from legal, it also was an emotive issue that brought Indian press under one umbrella. The discretionary provision of Indian Penal Code (1860), Indian Official Secrets Act (1889) and the Partition of Bengal were the events when the Indian press mounted sustained attack on the administration. These efforts brought prestige to the Indian press and it established itself as a force to reckon with.

The spirit of independence gradually became deep rooted in Hindi journals and their focused expression targeted towards achieving independence. The Vernacular Press Act could not prove to be deterrent enough to make language press fall in line as per wishes of the ruler. Therefore, other provisions were made in the Official Secrets Act in 1889. National Treason Act was promulgated to exercise the control more effectively. In 1910, Press Act was promulgated which required a guarantee money of ₹ 5000 from the printers of the newspaper. This was followed by the infamous Rowlatt Act. The Act promulgated in 1919 was like a fatal blow, and within 8–9 years of its existence, about 350 printing presses and 300 newspapers were tried in the court of law and finally shut down. About ₹ 6 lakhs were realized as penalty from the so-called defaulters (of the new acts). About 500 books were also confiscated and prevented from circulation. But the most fatal one was a new ordinance that was passed as Press and Unauthorised Newspapers Ordinance which brought even handbills and pamphlets under Government control.

Journey towards independence: The journey of press, especially Hindi press, was a difficult one in the beginning. The first Hindi newspaper was a weekly *Udant Martand* published from Calcutta on May 30, 1826. It was started by Pt. Yugal Kishore Shukla of Kanpur who was domiciled in Calcutta. On account of financial difficulty, the paper ceased publication on December 4, 1827.[41] There was a pathetic parting note by the editor in the last issue of the journal which said: The Sun (Udant Martand) has risen till today. But it's going to set, and set forever.* Raja Ram Mohan Roy came out with *Bangadoot*, first published on May 10, 1829. It was unique in the sense that it had contents in English, Bengali, Hindi and Persian. The first Hindi daily was *Samachar Sudhavarshan* that appeared in June, 1854 under the editorship of Shyamsunder Sen. The paper continued till 1868.[42]

---

* *आज दिवस लौ उग चुक्यौ मार्तण्ड उदन्त, अस्ताचल को जात है दिनकर दिन अब अंत ।*

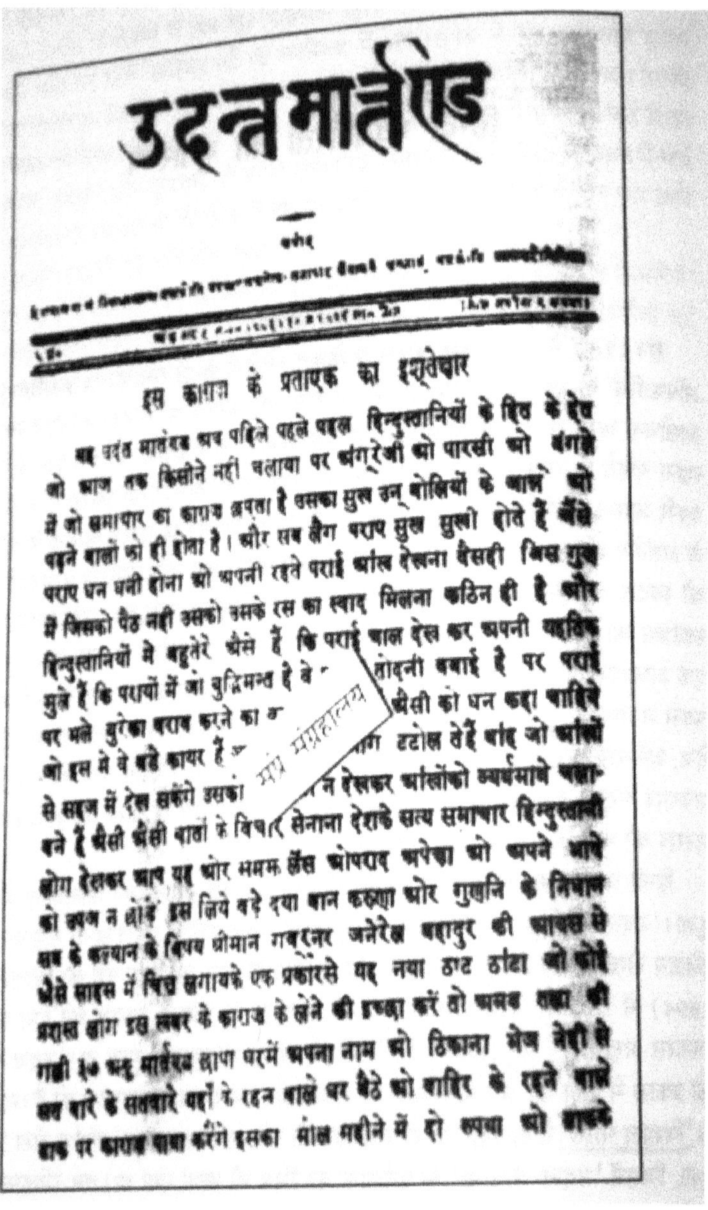

उदन्तमार्तण्ड

इस कागज के प्रताएक का इश्तेहार

Udant Martand: *First issue of the first Hindi newspaper, dated May 30, 1826, a weekly published from Calcutta. Photo credit: Sapre Sangrhalaya, Bhopal.*

The great revolt of 1857 gave a fillip to vernacular journalism in India in as much as it aroused the curiosity of educated classes to know about the developments which were taking place in the country in the wake of widespread revolt against the British Administration. The leaders of social reforms such as Dayanand Saraswati and Keshav Chandra Sen thought that the message of freedom could reach the masses through Hindi journalism, and so it should be encouraged. It was against this background that Hindi journalism flourished post 1857 and went on to become the most effective weapon in the Indian Independence movement.[43]

It (Hindi journalism) not only underlined but also explained in details the dangers of a foreign rule, its repercussion, its exploitation of masses in general and intelligentsia in particular. It could be safely said about Hindi journalism in early freedom struggle period that political leadership, journalism, and to a great extent, literature at that time presented an excellent synergy with the primary aim of establishing human values in the society.[44] Raja Ram Mohan Roy, Lokmanya Tilak, Lala Lajpat Roy, Chakraborthy Raj Gopalachari, Dr. Bhim Rao Ambedkar and Surendra Nath Banerjee were all wonderful communicators, apart from being statesmen. They chose the medium of journalism to express and to impress upon their views. Sentiments of equal intensity echoed in writings of editors of that time. Babu Rao Vishnu Paradkar, editor of *Aaj* (published from Benaras), had once said that he went to Calcutta not to become a journalist but to work closely with revolutionary committees and ensure freedom for the country by direct participation in the national freedom struggle.[45] Pt. Laxmikant Garde, editor of *Bharat Mitra,* also went on record to say that his entry into the field of journalism was directly influenced by the freedom struggle. Editor of *Vishal Bharat* Pt. Banarasi Das Chaturvedi resigned from his service from school to contribute freely and fearlessly to the cause of the freedom movement. Revolutionary literary figures like Makhan Lal Chaturvedi and Bal Krishna Sharma Naveen also preferred this medium to express their views. "I have consciously used the term Revolutionary literature, because of the fact that had they not got any medium to express their revolutionary instinct they would have certainly gone for direct intervention of a greater magnitude."[46] One of the most eminent among them was Ganesh Shankar Vidyarthi, who sacrificed his life for communal harmony, defined the policy of *Prabha* (edited by him) in these words:

> *"It'd be our endeavour to introduce our readers to each adverse and social conflict taking place internally or externally and help them to form their own opinion and invite them to debate welfare of the nation."*

Before that, *Pratap* in its inaugural issue while elaborating on its policies said, "*Pratap* enters its karma-kshetra (field of activity) with great hope, aspiration and belief in its objective. Our objective is welfare of entire humanity and this objective could not fully be achieved without making India independent." *Pratap* carried one stanza of a Hindi poem below its mast which meant: Those who are not proud of themselves or are not proud of their motherland are not humans. They are like animals and like the dead ones.* While discussing its aims and objectives, *Aaj* from Benaras said, "Our aim is to attain independence in each and every sphere of life. Our aim is to enhance national pride, instill self-pride in citizens of India. We want our citizens to take utmost pride in being Indian rather than being hesitant about it. This pride could only come by worshipping the Goddess of independence."[47] In *Karmachari,* Makhanlal Chaturvedi explained the objective of the paper as, "We are *yogis* (ascetics) of Independence, *upasaks* (adorers) of *Mukti* (emancipation). An *upasak* of *mukti* will always disagree with slavery, be it slavery of body or mind or individuals or slavery of circumstances."

---

* *जिनको न निज गौरव तथा निज देश का अभिमान है, वह नर नहीं नर पशु निरा है और मृतक समान है.*

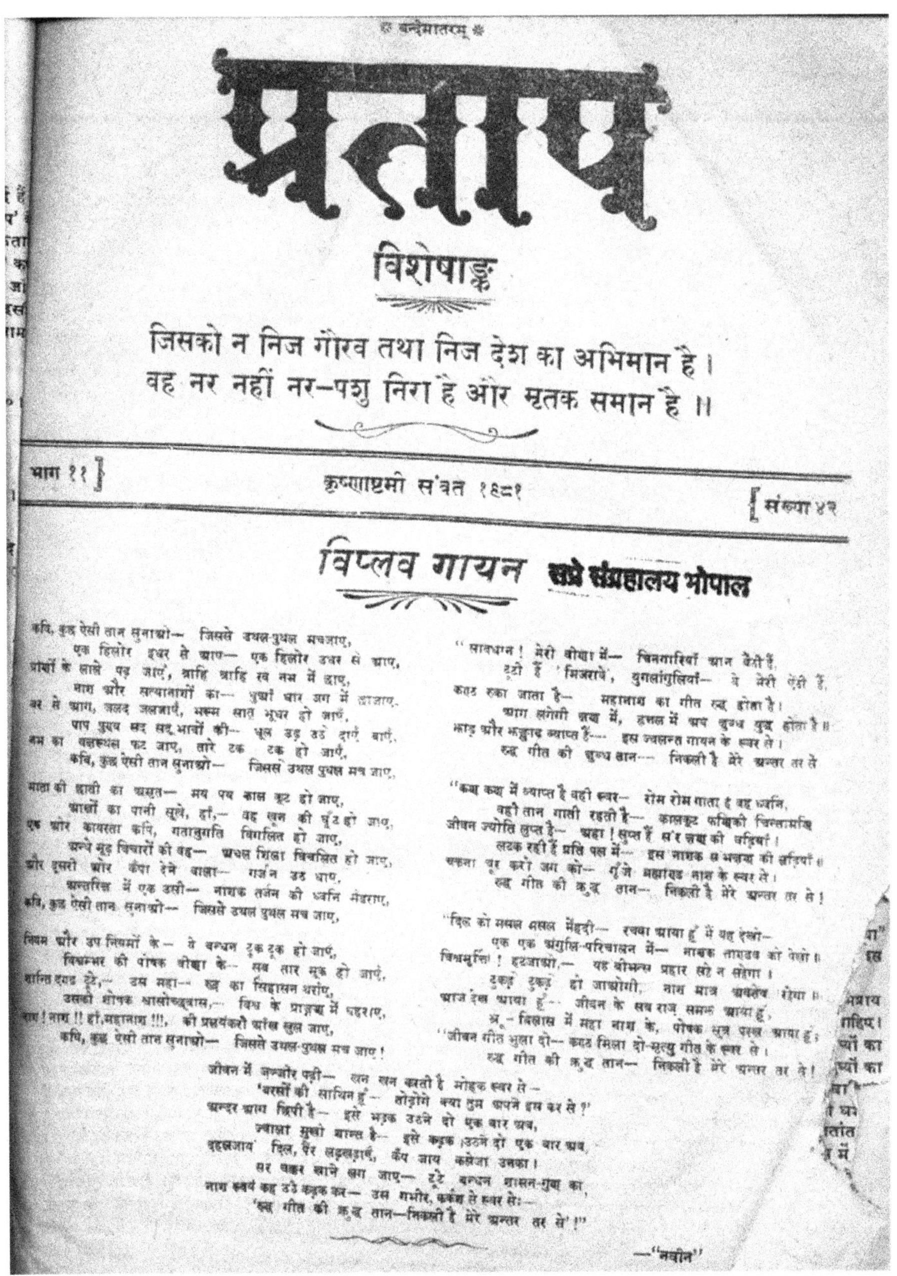

* वन्देमातरम् *

प्रताप

विशेषाङ्क

जिसको न निज गौरव तथा निज देश का अभिमान है।
वह नर नहीं नर-पशु निरा है और मृतक समान है॥

भाग ११] कृष्णाष्टमी संवत १९८१ [संख्या ४२

विप्लव गायन

सप्रे संग्रहालय भोपाल

कवि, कुछ ऐसी तान सुनाओ— जिससे उथल-पुथल मच जाए,
एक हिलोर इधर से आए— एक हिलोर उधर से आए,
प्राणों के लाले पड़ जाएँ, त्राहि त्राहि रव नभ में छाए,
नाश और सत्यानाशों का— धुआँधार जग में छा जाए,
बरसे आग, जलद जल जाएँ, भस्मसात भूधर हो जाएँ,
पाप पुण्य सद् सद् भावों की— धूल उड़ उठे दाएँ बाएँ,
नभ का वक्षस्थल फट जाए, तारे टूक टूक हो जाएँ,
कवि, कुछ ऐसी तान सुनाओ— जिससे उथल पुथल मच जाए,

माता की छाती का अमृत— मय पय कालकूट हो जाए,
आँखों का पानी सूखे, हाँ,— वह खून की घूँट हो जाए,
एक ओर कायरता काँपे, गतानुगति विगलित हो जाए,
अन्धे मूढ़ विचारों की वह— अचल शिला विचलित हो जाए,
और दूसरी ओर कँपा देने वाला— गर्जन उठ धाए,
अन्तरिक्ष में एक उसी— नाशक तर्जन की ध्वनि मँडराए,
कवि, कुछ ऐसी तान सुनाओ— जिससे उथल पुथल मच जाए,

नियम और उपनियमों के— ये बन्धन टूक टूक हो जाएँ,
विश्वम्भर की पोषक वीणा के— सब तार मूक हो जाएँ,
शान्ति दण्ड टूटे,— उस महा— रुद्र का सिंहासन थर्राए,
उसकी शोषक श्वासोच्छ्वास,— विश्व के प्राङ्गण में घहराए,
नाश ! नाश !! हाँ, महानाश !!!, की प्रलयंकरी आँख खुल जाए,
कवि, कुछ ऐसी तान सुनाओ— जिससे उथल-पुथल मच जाए !

"सावधान ! मेरी वीणा में— चिनगारियाँ आन बैठी हैं,
टूटी हैं मिजराबें, युगलांगुलियाँ— ये मेरी ऐंठी हैं,
कण्ठ रुका जाता है— महानाश का गीत रुद्ध होता है।
आग लगेगी क्षण में, हृत्तल में अब क्षुब्ध युद्ध होता है॥
झाड़ और झंखाड़ व्याप्त हैं— इस ज्वलन्त गायन के स्वर से।
रुद्ध गीत की क्षुब्ध तान— निकली है मेरे अन्तर तर से

"कण कण में व्याप्त है वही स्वर— रोम रोम गाता है वह ध्वनि,
वही तान गाती रहती है— कालकूट फणि की चिन्तामणि
जीवन ज्योति लुप्त है— अहा ! सुप्त हैं संरक्षण की घड़ियाँ !
लटक रही हैं प्रति पल में— इस नाशक संभक्षण की लड़ियाँ॥
चकनाचूर करो जग को— गूँजे ब्रह्माण्ड नाश के स्वर से।
रुद्ध गीत की क्रुद्ध तान— निकली है मेरे अन्तर तर से !

"दिल को मसल मसल मैंहदी— रचवा आया हूँ मैं यह देखो—
एक एक अंगुलि-परिचालन में— नाशक ताण्डव को देखो॥
विश्वमूर्त्ति ! हट जाओ,— यह बीभत्स प्रहार सहे न सहेगा।
टुकड़े टुकड़े हो जाओगी, नाम मात्र अवशेष रहेगा॥
आज देख आया हूँ— जीवन के सब राज़ समझ आया हूँ,
भ्रू-विलास में महा नाश के, पोषक सूत्र परख आया हूँ;
"जीवन गीत भुला दो— कण्ठ मिला दो-मृत्यु गीत के स्वर से।
रुद्ध गीत की क्रुद्ध तान— निकली है मेरे अन्तर तर से !

जीवन में झंकार पड़ी— खन खन करती है मोहक स्वर से—
'बरसों की साथिन हूँ— तोड़ोगे क्या तुम अपने इस कर से ?'
अन्दर आग छिपी है— इसे भड़क उठने दो एक बार अब,
ज्वाला मुखी शान्त है— इसे कड़क उठने दो एक बार अब,
दहल जाय दिल, पैर लड़खड़ाएँ, कँप जाय कलेजा उनका।
सर चक्कर खाने लग जाए— टूटे बन्धन शासन-गुण का,
नाश स्वयं कह उठे कड़क कर— उस गभीर, कर्कश से स्वर से:—
'रुद्ध गीत की क्रुद्ध तान—निकली है मेरे अन्तर तर से' !"

—"नवीन"

Front page of Pratap, Special issue dated Vikram Samvat 1981, i.e. 1925 Photo credit: Sapre Sangrhalaya, Bhopal.

Hans – edited by Munshi Premchand – was purely a literary magazine, but changed its tone and published a series of satirical pieces that exposed the colonial repressive tactics. All of these editors had some way or the other participated in the freedom struggle, served jail terms of different degrees and were victims of torture and repression. They became symbols of honesty and integrity and that's why they were taken seriously by readers. They never compromised with their ideologies and refused to bow down to the coercive tactics of the British. For these editors, it seemed that jail-term worked as a catalyst. When they returned to their desk after serving a jail-term, they resumed their attack on foreign rule with much more vigour and vitality. "There wasn't any language paper that surrendered and yielded to wishes of English rule. These editors became synonymous with the country's pride."[48] This generation of editors still remains the epitome of journalistic excellence and patriotism combined together.

Kesari (in Marathi) and *Maratha*[*] (in English), started by Lokmanya Tilak, were like harbingers in lighting the lamp of independence. It was exceptionally vocal in criticizing the perpetuation of repressive rule in India, so much so that its editor invited the wrath of the Raj. The British have recorded Bal Gangadhar Tilak as pioneer of "Garam Dal" *or*–hot faction or of extremist ideologies. "Naram Dal" or soft faction was led by Gopal Krishna Gokhale.[49] In 1908, when *Kesari* and *Maratha* were charged with treason, editor Lokmanya Tikak said, "despite Jury's decision, I am not guilty. May be it's His will that is more dear to me (to make India a free country) flourish in my pain and suffering rather than my comfort and independence. So be it."[50] There are not many instances in the history of Indian newspapers when an editor of a newspaper dared to challenge the ruling entity and preferably chose a path that invited

---

* *The building that housed the offices of Kesari in Pune still exists and contains the Tilak museum and Kesari-Maratha library. An online Marathi periodical called The Daily Kesari continues to be published, and is edited by his great grandson Deepak Tilak.*

nothing but direct confrontation. Naturally, such editors paid a heavy price for it, but they remained a lighthouse of inspiration for the entire journalistic fraternity for years to come. Hindi *Kesari* was started in 1908 by publisher Dr. Balkrishna Shriram Munje. It reproduced content from original Marathi into Hindi. The famous write-up for which *Kesari* was charged with treason was also published in the Hindi edition. For some time thereafter, the Hindi edition of *Kesari* was closed.[51]

The purpose of Indian journalism during the freedom struggle was mainly aimed at inculcating self-pride and consciousness so that the dormant power embedded in every Indian could be awakened. The mission statement of *Kesari* was more direct and was like a wake-up call for the rulers. It said, "*Savdhan, Jab desh ki praja neend se jaag jayegee tab tumhari khair nahin* (Beware, you wouldn't be spared when citizens of the country come out of their slumber)".[52] The opinion and views expressed in those newspapers reflected the public sentiment fervently. The basic consciousness of newspapers in general was an extension of the basic consciousness shown by *Kesari* and *Maratha*.[53] This was the tone that was overtly/ covertly maintained by journalism in those times. *Kesari* issued a directive to its Delhi bureau in which it said, "we at *Kesari* do not write for rulers, we write to ensure safety and peace of our citizen, to instill encouragement (in the people of the country) is the prime duty of a (Indian) journalist. And precisely this is what we will be doing at *Kesari*."

Bhartendu Harishchandra started three publications: *Kavi Vachan Sudha, Harischandra Magazine* and *Harischandra Chandrika*. And the era of nationalist journalism began. "Nationalist because their content reflected, nurtured and spread the concept of Swadeshi. They were so pure and honest in their approach and attitude that it organized political leaders around this concept and established the freedom movement as an effective literary power as well."[54] *Kavi Vachansudha* in its issue dated March 23, 1928, published an appeal to boycott imported cloth. It said:

> *"From today onwards we won't wear foreign clothes. Clothes purchased earlier would be used till its old enough to discard. But no new foreign cloth would be purchased. We will proudly wear Indian clothes." Bhartendu's passion for Swadeshi irked the colonial rulers. They treated it as a type of treason and the government adverts to the newspaper was stopped. In response, Bhartendu returned the honorary magistracy given to him by the British Government.*[55]

Bhartendu's contemporary Pt. Bal Krishna Bhatt started a monthly journal *Hindi* Hindi *Pradeep*. It has the credit of being the first literary monthly dedicated to nationalist ideologies. But, after 1875 it became more revolutionary in its tone. Publication of *Hindi Pradeep* was followed by other publications like *Bharat Mitra* in 1878, *Hindustan* in 1887 and *Bangwasi* in 1890. *Bangwasi* was the first newspaper that raised its voice against the consent bill. *Hindustan** under the editorship of Pt. Madan Mohan Malviya and Balmukund Gupta played an important role in the promotion of national consciousness. *Bharat Mitra* in one of its issues fearlessly criticized the British Policy of exporting grains from India and termed it creation of an equivalent of food crisis in the country. Hindi journalism in those days debated on topical issues, raised serious concerns about public interest subjects and exposed the colonial repression. Thus, newspapers aroused public interest in day- to-day happenings and helped immensely in creating an environment against the British rule in India. People started taking keen interest in political and social issues. It

* *Pt. Madan Mohan Malviya laid the foundation of two newspapers named Hindustan. The first Hindustan was published with the help of the Raja Rampal Singh of Kalakankar estate (Pratapgarh, UP) in 1883. When Pt. Malviya associated himself with Hindustan Times, he launched Hindustan in 1936. Hindustan from Kalakankar could not survive for long. But Hindustan launched in 1936 is the same Hindustan published by Hindustan Media Ventures Ltd, Delhi having multiple editions from Bihar, UP, Jharkhand and Uttarakhand, apart from Delhi/NCR. It went on to become one the most authentic and celebrated newspapers having the largest market- share (as much as 75 per cent in case of Bihar) in Hindi-speaking states of Bihar, UP and Jharkhand.*

clearly indicated towards a future that was going to be tough on English rulers. *Saarsudhanidhi* in its issue dated July 12, 1880 stressed the need for representative system of governance in India in one of its articles.[56] This was the first attempt to establish parliamentary democracy as the only alternative for sovereignty in India. Apart from serious approaches like these, the negative impact of colonial governance like taxes, famines were bitterly criticized. Leaders writing were being written in these issues of newspapers and literary magazines, and also published poetries and essays. Even satires and humour pieces targeted the repressive rule. Two satirical pieces by Bhartendu Harischandra in *Harishchandra Chandrika* are worth mentioning. One was *Angrezon Se Hindustaniyon ka jee kyon nahin Milta* and other was *Kaliraj Ki Sabha*. These two satirical pieces came down heavily on rulers and their supporters.

In one, Bhartendu compared rulers with gluttons and the ruled one with the victim. It seems satire was chosen as the preferred medium to avoid direct confrontation with the Vernacular Press Act. But the tone and inherent message was quite clear to the Indian readers. The anger embedded in these different formats of communication was so focused against the colonial rule that it laid down the path for a larger future revolt and freedom struggle. Journalism at that time expressed its opinion against Ilbert Bill of1884, Consent Bill of 1891 and Indian Council Act of 1892, and by confronting with such issues of national importance, journalism on its own accord embraced a national outlook.[57]

Another turning point in Indian journalism was the formation of the Indian National Congress in 1885. The Indian National Congress, also known as the Congress Party, comprised chiefly of members of the Western-educated professional elite. Public opinion had started to turn against the British Government and it sought to represent the views of the populace from both urban and rural areas. There was an undercurrent of feeling that British rule was unfair, and this is reflected in the newspaper reports contained in a separate chapter in the book. Agitation and disturbances in the streets were common, and the media played a huge role in re-enforcing feelings of real and imagined grievances.[58] But this coincided with the Partition of Bengal, which attracted strong reactions from people in general and different classes in particular. This paved the way for a separate extremist ideology in Indian journalism.

The nation was abuzz with revolutionary activities. For Hindi journalism, Lokmanya Tilak became the ideal, and simultaneously newspapers and journals like *Karmayogi, Swaraj, Abhyuday*, *Pratap* and *Kesari* – all having a revolutionary tone – focused on informing the readers of repression and atrocities of the Raj. Collectively, it all helped in creating an environment against the rulers and informing and educating the masses of the repression and atrocities. The total impact was deep enough and "words of newspaper were considered as sacrosanct as that of Geeta, Quran and Bible."[59] The press in cities such as Agra, Lucknow, Kanpur, Oudh, Allahabad and Benares played a significant role in the growth of nationalism after the Indian National Congress was formed in 1885. Improvements in education fostered the exchange of ideas and aspirations for liberty from the foreign rule. Though literacy was as low as 10–11 per cent [compared to 75 per cent of today], but people were quite sensitive to issues related to their country's freedom. So, printed news used to reach through word-of- mouth mode to a larger number, and the sound of revolt reverberated in the air of the entire country. It was so intense that Simon Commission in its report considered it as a serious threat, and since then, journalists, printing press and newspapers came under the more direct scanner of the Government.[60]

वर्ष १. पुणें:—मंगळवार तारीख ४ जानेवारी १८८१. अंक १.

First Issue of Kesari

First issue of Kesari, dated 4 January 1881, edited by Bal Gangadhar Tilak. Photo credit: Mumbai Heritage

Other means of mass media like the radio was under full control of British Government and was used as propaganda machinery for them. Newspapers, under various pressures from the Government, had to face dire consequences for criticizing and reporting governmental apathy. But such punishment could hardly prove to be a deterrent; rather they injected fresh vigor, and publications started in different dialects also. Bihar saw a huge influx of publications from different districts in different dialects like Bhojpuri, Magahi and Maithili – apart from Hindi and English.[61] *Aaj* from Benaras proved to be an asset in spreading the message of Gandhi as his thoughts, his ideas and his opinions were given ample space in the paper. Such work done with a missionary zeal not only touched millions of hearts but also helped them to inform and educate about the freedom movement, importance of Swadeshi and achieving the goal through non-violence. *Aaj* used *Navjeevan, Harijan* and *Young India* as its basis for spreading the message of Gandhi.[62] The concept of swadeshi was gaining popularity and to express this concept in its entirety, a separate publication *Swadesh* was launched in 1919 with its first issue hitting the stand on April 6. The paper had a Hindi stanza below its mast which meant that people with no emotion and without the flow of (sap of) life, have hearts made of stone where love for the country does not exist.[*]

Such messages on the front pages of newspapers certainly had a positive impact on the general psyche of the readers and an undercurrent of nationalism started flowing through the length and breadth of the country.

Pt. Jhabarmall Sharma wrote in *Calcutta Samachar* — Indians have realized their inherent potential like that of Hanuman and unleashing of this huge potential could neither be stopped by Governor of Bengal nor Colonel Beadon's elder brother Sir O'Dyer.[63]

Aaj dedicated itself to the national cause, and it inspired the publication of other dailies. *Vartman* from Kanpur (November 23, 1920)

---

* *भरा नहीं भावों से, बहती जिसमें रसधार नहीं, हृदय नहीं वह पत्थर है जिसमें स्वदेश का प्यार नहीं.*

was another paper fully dedicated to the cause of nationalist movement and the ideals of Gandhi. In its issue dated January 26, 1921, *Vartman* published an appeal to the youth of the country in which it said, "If you are a true son (of your soil), be like Prahalaad and free me (your motherland) from all my miseries and pain by peaceful and moralistic means." *Pratap* in its issue dated August 22, 1921 under the title "*Swaraj Lena*" (having swaraj) wrote, "Let (them) pass Rowlett act in thousands; let (them) repeat Jalianwala massacre millions of time and let (them even) lock our tongues – but finally we will have swaraj."[64]

Partition of Bengal and massacre of Jalianwala Bagh – these two incidents triggered dissent in general, but Gandhi's influence of peaceful struggle was so overpowering that even an aggressive newspaper like *Pratap* appealed to its readers in its editorial for a greater restraint, "Let them perpetuate the tyranny, but neither our behaviour should reflect any violent reaction nor should we be deviated from our main aims and objectives. We should remain firmly rooted where ever we are. Ultimately, the message of our ultimate victory will arrive."[65]

Editors like Pt. Sundar Lal, Ganesh Shankar Vidyarthi, Makhan Lal Chaturvedi, Bal Krishna Sharma 'Navin' expressed their revolutionary sentiments in their poetries. "*Desh Bhakt, Ham Kranti Karenge, Jeevan Sangram, Ghabrate Kyon Ho, Vijay, Maa*" were some of the phrases that were often reflected in editorials and edit-page articles, apart from poetries and features. Special issues were brought out to spread the revolutionary message. *Vijay Ank* of *Swadesh*, *Phansi Ank* of *Chand* and *Jhanda Satyagraha Ank* of *Prabha* have all become compilations of historical importance. Hindi journalism sensed the spirit of our constitution much earlier. The farmers' agitation of the 1920's, labor union activities, communist ideologies, Russian Revolution, Life and Time of Marx and Lenin were some of the topics that were frequently discussed at great lengths in Hindi newspapers.[66] The newspapers not only informed and educated about socialist thoughts but also expressed their commitment to this form of governance. When Lenin died in 1924,

Aaj, Vartman, Prabha, Saraswati and *Madhuri* paid special tributes by publishing write-ups about the leader. When socialism entered Indian journalism, it hugely impacted political thoughts at that time. This gave a momentum to Indian struggle of independence, giving it a more solid and concrete form.[67]

"If Indian farmers, labourers and peasants believed for the first time, that other countries trying for independence were equally concerned about the independence of this country, and that the independence is directly related to prosperous future of country's citizens, credit for this ought to be given to Hindi Journalism. Hopes and aspirations were raised and it was felt that independence should be attained even if lives were to be sacrificed."[68]

This was the time when Urdu patriotic poem written by Bismil Azimabadi as an ode to young freedom fighters of India emerged: Sarfaroshii kii tamannaa ab hamaare dil mein hai/ Dekhnaa hai zor kitnaa baazu-e-qaatil mein hai: The desire to sacrifice is now in our heart, we shall see how much strength is there in the arms of our assassin.*

Increasing pressure of pre-censorship and other repressive measures necessitated editors to organize so that a solution could be found out through a common platform. In 1894, Hindi Uddharini Pratinidhi Sabha was formed which graduated into the Press Association of India in 1915. Other organizations were also formed and editors' conferences were convened. The unity bubbling with the organizational strength raised the fighting spirit of the Hindi press. Now, it was in a position to negotiate a certain degree of independence with responsible journalism, making the entire press more impactful.

---

* *सरफरोशी की तमन्ना अब हमारे दिल में है, देखना है ज़ोर कितना बाजुए क़ातिल है: This is sometimes wrongly attributed to Ram Prasad Bismil. Revolutionary Ram Prasad Bismil faced the gallows uttering these powerful words.*

Since the beginning of the 1930s till independence, the movements that took place around the country were well publicized by the Hindi press, and it played a key role in informing and educating the country. Whether it was boycott of Simon Commission (1928) or Salt Satyagraha (1930) or the Quit India Movement of 1942, newspapers of that era presented Hindi journalisms in best of its forms, suitably complemented by actions on political fronts.[69] Also, the Hindi press was more vocal now and was able to put more uncomfortable questions to the administration. *Aaj* in its issue dated April 8, 1930, announced with regard to the breaking of Salt Law, "long awaited struggle for independence has begun." After breaking the Salt Law, the paper wrote, "now time has come, this law should be broken in each and every Indian household."

By the beginning of the Quit India Movement, colonial rulers had to review the limited independence given to the Indian press. They came down heavily on the language press – publication of *Aaj* and *Pratap* were suspended and copies of *Harijan* were confiscated. At these critical times, mode of expression shifted to college magazines from that of newspapers.[70] *Central Hindu College Magazine* from Benares is specially mentioned in British Records with a circulation figure of 5,500 copies monthly – a huge circulation figure in those days. Kumar Kalika Prasad Singh, nephew of Maharaja Ravaneshwar Singh of Gidhdhur and a student of the college, was the first person to be charged under section 170 of CRPC in Bihar as leader of the non-cooperation movement and was awarded one-year imprisonment. Trial began on October 16, 1921 and sentencing was done on October 22, 1921. Kumar turned down suggestions of non-complicity. This was prominently covered in Mahatma Gandhi's *Young India* under the caption "The temperance of work a crime". Later *The Searchlight* published a letter written by Kalika Prasad Singh in which he cleared his stand and explained why he did not bow down to coercive tactics of the administration.[71]

Payam-e-Azadi started publication in Hindi and Urdu in 1857. It called upon the people to fight against the British. The paper was soon confiscated and anyone found with a copy of the paper was prosecuted for sedition. *Doorbeen* and *Sultan-ul-Akbar* published in Urdu and Persian respectively were tried for publishing a 'Firman' by Bahadur Shah Zafar urging people to drive the British out of India. *Hindi Patriot*, established in 1853, published a play *Neel Darpan* in 1861, which focused on exploitation of indigo workers and urged people to stop cultivation of indigo crop for white masters. This created a movement of the sort.[72]

How journalism and nationalist politics were interwoven into one another is quite apparent from the fact that when the first ever meeting of Congress was held in Mumbai, in 1885, some of the prominent members were editors of newspapers and journals. The first ever resolution proposed to Congress was moved by the editor of *The Hindu*, G. Subramanian Ayer. In this resolution, it was demanded that the Government should appoint a committee to enquire into the functioning of the Indian administration. The second resolution was also moved by a journalist from Poona – V K Chiplunkar. He was co- founder of *Kesari* and *Maratha* with Bal Gangadhar Tilak in which the Congress was urged to demand abolition of India Council which ruled the country from Britain. The third resolution was supported and fourth was proposed by Dada Bhai Naoroji. He had started a Zoroastrian fortnightly *Rast Goftar* (truth teller)[73].

(During his visit to England in 1855 he delivered a series of lectures and wrote many articles for the press to educate the British people about their Government's responsibilities as rulers of India.)

Hasan Imam, an associate of *The Searchlight*, was called upon to preside over a special session of the Indian National Congress held in Bombay from August 28 to September 1918 to consider the Montagu- Chelmsford Report. Hasan Imam and Mazharul Haque were among prominent leaders of India who called upon Montagu, Secretary of State for India, on November 26, 1917, along with the Congress and Home Rule deputation. Montagu described them as real giants of the Indian political world. Regarding the meeting he wrote, "We were face-to-face with the real giants of Indian Political World. We had not these dupes and adherents from the provinces, but we had a collection of first class politicians of various provinces. Old Surendranath Banerjee, the veteran from Bengal, read the address, which was beautifully written and beautifully read. There was Mudholker from the Central Provinces, Jinnah from Bombay, Mazhrul Haque and Hasan Imam from Bihar and Orissa, Gandhi, Mrs. Besant, Vasav Pillai and so on. All the brains of the .3movement were there."[74]

Hasan Imam handled the situation that averted a head-on collision between the Extremists (led by Lok Manya Tilak) and Moderates very deftly. Hasan Imam told the gathering that there was no material difference between those who advocated rejection of reform proposals and those who advised their acceptance as the aim of both was to continue the struggle till our rights were won. The names "Extremist" and "Moderate" had been designed by our enemies to divide them. [75]

There were many Congress presidents who had either been the editors or had started publication of one or the other newspapers. In this context, particular mention may be made of Feroze Shah Mehta who had started the *Bombay Chronicle* and Pt. Madan Mohan Malaviya who edited the daily *Hindustan*. He also extended help in the publication of *Leader* from Allahabad. Moti Lal Nehru was the first Chairman of the Board of Directors of the *Leader*. Lala Lajpat Rai inspired the publication of three journals: the *Punjabi*, *Vandematram* and the *People* from Lahore. Subhash Chandra Bose and C.R. Das were not journalists but they acquired the papers like *Forward* and *Advance*, which later attained national status.[76] Jawaharlal Nehru founded the *National Herald*. In case of the revolutionary movement, it can be safely said that it did not begin with guns and bombs but it started with the publication of newspapers.[77] The first to be mentioned in this context is *Jugantar* publication started by Barindra Kumar Ghosh who also edited it. After *Jugantar*, it was *Vandematram* that played a significant role in the freedom struggle. This journal was established by Subodh Chandra Malik, C.R. Das and

Bipin Chandra Pal on August 6, 1906., Aurobindo Ghosh, the editor of *Sandhya*, B. Upadhyay and editor of *Jugantar*, B. N. Dutt, had to a face a trial for espousing the cause of freedom. Some other notable publications were *Uchit Vakta*, a weekly from Calcutta. It appeared on August 7, 1880 and was founded and initially edited by Pt. Durga Prasad Mishra. It adopted a policy of opposing the Government and championed the cause of Swadeshi and national integration. It survived till 1895.[78] *Hindi Bangavasi* was founded as a weekly in 1890 and edited by Pt. Amritlal Chakravarty till 1900. He was succeeded by Pt. Ambika Prasad Bajpai. At a later stage a daily was also published from this house. Its annual subscription was ₹ 2 and the subsidized rate was possible because it had a common establishment with its Bengali counterpart; it reached 2,000 subscribers in its early stage. It was published regularly until about the mid-1930s. This paper was a training ground for a number of Hindi journalists who made their mark at one time or the other.[79] Among them Balmukund Gupta, Baburao Vishnu Paradkar, Pt. Ambika Prasad Bajpai and Lakshmi Narayan Garde may specially be mentioned. This paper also introduced pictures for the first time in Hindi journalism to illustrate events and personalities. *Nrisingh* was a monthly magazine which appeared in 1907 from Calcutta and was edited and managed by Pt. Ambika Prasad Bajpai, and was solely devoted to politics. But it could survive only for a year. *Devanagar* was founded by Mr. Justice Sharda Charan Mitra and published in Devanagari script. The object of the founder was to facilitate assimilation of news. He advocated only one script, namely Devanagari, for all the Indian languages. *Vishwamitra*, a daily newspaper founded and edited by Mulchand Agarwal, first appeared towards the end of 1915.[80] In the life-time of its founder, it began to be published simultaneously from Calcutta, Bombay, Kanpur and Patna, and is still continuing.

On account of faster means of communication, trade and commerce, the world had become revolutionized, and therefore, the mercantile community of Calcutta – as indeed elsewhere –wanted to have the latest news about prices ruling in the commercial capitals of the world. The late Mulchand Agarwal, who hailed from a mercantile community, immediately sensed the situation and based the news of his paper on the telegrams from the international news agencies, and thus brought out a revolution in Hindi journalism. *Bharat Mitra* and *Calcutta Samachar* failed in the race for early news and had to close down. *Swatantra* appeared as a daily on August 4, 1920 and was edited by Pt. Ambika Prasad Bajpai who had left *Bharat Mitra* in 1919. It was popular among the businessmen on account of commercial intelligence which it printed. It also published national views of the Gandhian era.

Matwala[*] – a novel experiment – appeared as a weekly on August 26, 1923 was the only paper of its kind in Hindi which presented news and views in a novel literary style based on wits, satire and cartoons. In the very first year of its existence, it began to publish 10,000 copies[81] (the circulation figure was huge for that period). Its editorial board had three great literary figures, namely Shivapujan Sahay, Munshi Navajadiklal Shrivastava and Pt. Suryakant Tripathi 'Nirala'. The management side was looked after by Mahadeva Prasad Seth, who owned the press. It sold 2,000 copies even in Benaras where a local daily *Aaj*, founded by Shiva Prasad Gupta, had a dominating position. *Matwala* brought out a revolution in Hindi journalism, but could not survive for long.

Shrikrishna Sandesh came out in 1925 and was edited by Pt. Lakshmi Narayan Garde. It was devoted to politics but had a distinct literary style. However, it was also very short-lived. Lack of subscribers and paucity of patrons was the usual weakness of Hindi papers of the period (1825–1925). Literacy among the mercantile community from the up-country was poor. It is said that Pt. Durga Prasad Mishra, who was really

---

* *Matwala carried these lines below its mast-* अमिय-गरल-शशि-शीकर रविकर/राग-विराग भरा प्याला/पीते हैं जो साधक उनका प्यारा है मतवाला *(Matwala talks about its reader's profile, it says, "those who love this paper are like an ascetic who embrace the good, the bad, the attachment and the detachment uniformly. Without any hesitation or discrimination."*

the mainspring behind most of the Hindi journals of the last century, used to visit the *gaddi* of merchants of Bara Bazar, Calcutta and read the contents of news to businessmen to make them interested in newspapers. However, it appears that his missionary zeal was seldom reciprocated by the constituents whom he aimed to serve.[82]

From all over India, one after another newspapers and magazines were being published. Some were not so successful. It was as if a *yajna* was being performed, *yajna* of independence in which everyone had to sacrifice his share. Compilation of the newspapers and magazines started by freedom fighters would make the picture clearer. *Som Prakash* (1858, Ishwar Chandra Vidyasagar), *Indian Mirror* (1862, Devendra Nath Tagore), *Amrit Bazar Patrika* (1868, Sisir Kumar Ghosh and Motilal Ghosh), *Tehzib-ul-Akhlaq* (1871, Journal, Sir Syed Ahmed Khan), *Kesari* (1881,Marathi, Bal Gangadhar Tilak), *Prabuddha Bharat* (1896, English Monthly, P. Aiyaswami on behest of Swami Vivekananda), *Udbodhan* (1899, Bangla Magaazine, Swami Vivekananda) *Bande Mataram* (1905, English, Aurobindo Ghosh), *Jugantar Patrika* (1906, the short-lived revolutionary paper was started by Barindra Kumar Ghosh, Avinash Bhattachrya and Bhupendra Dutta in 1906, but was forced to close down in 1908)* *Bombay Chronicle* (1910, English, Firoz Shah Mehta), *New India* (1914, English, Annie Besant), *Independent* (1919, Motilal Nehru), *Mook Nayak* (1920, Marathi Weekly, BR Ambedkar), *Hindustan Times* (inaugurated by Mahatma Gandhi in 1923), *Hindustan* (1936, Madan Mohan Malviya,). Please refer to a detailed list of newspapers and journals in Appendix III.

मूकनायक

बहिष्कृत भारत

सुबोध वचनें

आजकालचे प्रश्न

مسلمان

THE MUSALMAN

MUSTAFA
GOLD MART

Fathima
JEWELLERS

Mook Nayak (1920) & Bahishkrit Bharat (1927): Two journals edited by Dr. B R Ambedkar. Photo credit: Wikimedia Cosmos and The Musalman (below), edited by Syed Azmatullah, It has been called preservation of a dream, from a beginning in 1927, pages are still filled by Calligraphers. Photo credit: Coca-cola india stories: https://www.coca- colaindia.com/stories/lbr-2019-the-only-handwritten-newspaper.

Ghadar – a call for mutiny in India from abroad: Ghadar movement has been largely erased from the popular collective narrative. When discussing the impact of newspaper on India, the story of *Ghadar* needs to be told separately for several reasons. **One**, it educated Indians about British exploitations (published reports on revenue earned by British Government from India and its per capita spending for the country).

Two, it educated on ways to channelize energy and stamina for a greater cause of independence rather than wasting it in attaining sectarian goals. **Three,** it educated Indians about prioritizing their goal rather than asking for Hindi or Urdu to be given their rightful place (it indicated that asking them, the foreign ruler, to decide our language is like contemplating that they will be here forever, and that is certainly not the case).

Four, it propagated the view that abolition of sati and other social evils are good – but 800,000 people died of plague and 20 million died of famine during the last 10 years. It was not because of any social evil but because of the apathy of a foreign rule. All our evils can be well taken care of once we are free. Not being free in one's own country exerts extreme moral, physical and emotional stress. It appealed to Indians to rise above narrow sectarian goals and fight for the freedom of the country.

The publication of *Ghadar* was unique in the sense that it reflected genuine thirst for freedom, with honesty and integrity in its intellectual output. *Ghadar* was a group that handled 22 different publications altogether in four different Indian languages[83],and also released numerous pamphlets and other materials that vigorously propagated the cause of Indian independence among Indian expatriates living in the US, Canada and other parts of the world. The paper was distributed to Politico-Indian centers in United States, Canada, Philippines, Fiji, Sumatra, Japan, Shanghai, Hong Kong, Java, Singapore, Malaya, Siam, Burma, India and East Africa. Copies came to India as well.[84]

The US *Ghadar* was first published in Urdu on November 1, 1913, in Gurumukhi on December 8, 1913 and later in Hindi on March 1, 1914.

It became one of the most important milestones in the Indian struggle for independence. It emphasized the point that, "56 years have passed since the last mutiny of 1857, another one is due." The language of the paper was bitter, pungent and vitriolic.[85]

The inaugural issue of *Ghadar* announced on the right side of the page under the title –*Our Work, Our Name*. It declared:

> *"Today on November 1, 1913, a new calendar is launched in the history of India. From now onward, a war against the British Rule is initiated from a foreign land in our native languages. It is an auspicious occasion that a paper in Urdu and Gurumukhi is launched to uproot the British from India."*[48] *Lala Hardayal was the editor of the first issue and the Urdu translation was done by Vishveshwar Parsad of U.P. In his inaugural Address, Hardayal said: "In the history of today's India, a new era is set in motion. The power of 'PEN' will explode like a ball of cannon. This newspaper is the staunch enemy of the English Empire and a bugle of challenge for the Indian youth. Wake up, take up arm and fight for the independence of India."*[86]

In the editorial challenging questions were posed and answered therein. It declared its aims and objectives as:

- **What** is our name? Ghadar, Mutiny.
- **What** is our work? Ghadar, Mutiny
- **Where** will the mutiny take place? In India
- **When**? In a few years
- **Why**? Because the people can no longer bear the tyranny and oppression of the British rule and are anxious to fight and diefor freedom.

Occasionally *Ghadar* used to publish the following advertisement:

Wanted: Enthusiastic and heroic soldiers for organizing Ghadar in Hindustan:

Renumeration: Death

Reward- Martyrdom

Pension: Freedom

Field of work: Hindustan.

Ghadar worked as an epicenter of activities around which immigrant Indians came together for a common cause. It included intellectuals and immigrant Indian workers as well. People associated with *Ghadar* publication came to be known as Ghadrites or people of Ghadar party. Many Indians – mostly Sikhs – had migrated to Canada and the US in search of jobs. This surge in Hindu immigration annoyed Canadian authorities. Indians were totally banned in Canada by 1909. In 1914, Komagata Maru, the ship carrying Indians, reached Vancouver port, but only 27 were admitted to Canada and the rest were not allowed out of the ship. More than 300 Punjabi immigrants were forced out of British Columbia (Canada) on July 24, 1914 after more than sixty days of day-and-night struggle in Vancouver, mainly due to racist reasons. The ship sailed towards Calcutta via Hong Kong. While it was nearing Calcutta, on September 26, 1914, the Imperial Indian Police intercepted the ship and tried to arrest group leaders. It was confronted by passengers and the police opened fire. 20 passengers were shot dead in indiscriminate firing. Many others were taken into custody.[87] Komagata Maru incident – from its refusal in July to enter Canadian waters and their receptionby indiscriminate firing in the end of homeward journey – was a triggerpoint to start a pan-India rebellion by Ghadarites. It inspired thousands of Indian immigrants to come back and organize an armed rebellionagainst British imperialism. Indian students in American universities were quite concerned with the happenings in Canada. They felt an urgent need to disseminate information about the plight of Indians, especially among Indians living in the US and Canada. One of the students Tarak Nath Das started the publication of *Free Hindustan* in 1908 from Vancouver, British

Columbia. This was followed by publication of *Swadesh Sevak* in 1909 by Gurudatta Kumar. Shyamji Krishna Verma started publishing *Indian Sociologist* in London. Lala Hardayal, who was teaching in California University, Berkley, was a central point of movements related to Indian independence abroad.[88] The Pacific Coast Hindustan Association was formed with its head office in San Francisco. The building from which operation of the association was conducted was named Jugantar Ashram (after the famous revolutionary Bengali paper *Jugantar*). The following information is from the record of Stockton, California Gurdwara Library. Many members of the Ghadar party visited, and some even lived at the Stockton Gurdwara prior to 1930.

Ghadar Di gunj-special issue of Ghaderite folk patriotic songs that was reprinted on demand, Courtesy:Page URL:https://commons.wikimedia.org/wiki/File:Ghadar_di_ gunj.jpg,FileURL:https://upload.wikimediaorg/wikipedia/commons/5/51/Ghadar_di_gunj.jpg.

Founding members of Ghadar were:

- Sohan Singh Bhakhna (President)
- Kesar Singh (Vice President)
- Lala Hardayal (General Secretary & Editor, Urdu Ghadar)
- Kartar Singh Sarabha (Editor, Punjabi Ghadar)
- Baba Jawala Singh (Vice President)
- Baba Vaisakha Singh
- Balwant Singh
- Pt. Kanshi Ram (Treasurer)
- Harnam Singh Tundilat
- G. D. Verma
- Lala Thaker Das (Dhuri) (Vice Secretary)
- Munshi Ram (Organizing Secretary)
- Bhai Parmanand
- Nidhan Singh Chugha
- Santokh Singh
- Master Udham Singh 17.
- Baba Harnam Singh (Kari Sari)
- Karim Baksh
- Amar Chand
- Rehmat Ali
- Vishnu Ganesh Pingle (et al.)

Lala Hardayal, Raghubar Dayal and Kartar Singh Sarabha (who looked after printing and production) were key players in making *Ghadar* viable till 1917. The dedication of the team behind it made *Ghadar* an instant hit with the Indian audience abroad. As stated earlier, the aim of *Ghadar* was to keep the spirit of 1857 alive. It advocated armed revolution and open revolt against the British, and appealed to Indians living abroad to return to their motherland and fight for the country's independence. The weekly serialized the famous book by Savarkar *Bhartiya Swatantrata Ka Pratham Yudh* in its various issues. *Ghadar* also carried folk songs that reflected hope and aspirations of the Indian people for a free India. Special issues, namely *Ghadar di Goonj,* has been preserved in South Asian American Digital Archive (SAADA). Goonj's songs became immensely popular, and a special edition containing these songs were reprinted on readers' demand and distributed separately from the main paper.[89] Several students from India in those days were studying in University of California at Berkeley; majority of them from Bengal and Punjab. They were potential revolutionaries who needed a mass base. When the turbulence amongst the Indian workers came to their notice, they flocked to work with them at once. How the tide was turned and countless Indian workers became Ghadarites in a short time can be understood from Baba Sohan Singh Bakhna's account of those days.[90] "The standard of living of the American worker was higher than that of immigrant workers. They would decline to work on low wages. Besides, they got unemployment allowance. But the Asian workers, mostly from Japan, China, India, Turkey and Russia were hard-pressed and had to work on low wages. The American workers, somehow, got convinced that the Indian immigrants were threat to safety and security of their jobs. They attacked the Indian workers at night and beat them up after looting their belongings. This happened five to six times. Once, Indian workers were forcibly loaded into streetcars, driven to the wilderness of the forest and left there. The victims approached the English counselor for redressal of the grievance but to no avail. One such attack was organized by the American workers against the Japanese workers. The latter complained to their Government which took such a serious cognizance of the situation that the American Government had to pay compensation and assure the Japanese of protection in the future. It dawned upon us Indians that since we were slaves in our own homeland nobody cared for us, and there could be no redressal to the situation unless we became free as a people."

Indians living abroad responded in thousands to the emotional appeal of *Ghadar* to return to their motherland for an armed struggle and open revolt against the British Empire in India. A pan-Indian rebellion was planned by Ghadrites. The time was cautiously chosen as the British became engaged in one of the deadliest conflict of humanity, i.e., the First World War (1914–1918). February 20, 1915 was the D-day. British military informers had successfully infiltrated the movement and before the planned revolt could erupt, there was massive round up of Ghadarites not only in India but from around the world. Lala Hardayal moved to Germany to avoid arrest. Kartar Singh Sarabha returned to his village via Colombo. Some sources indicate that on his way home with Sohan Singh Bakhna, Kartar Singh Sarabha met passengers of the Komagatu Maru ship at the port of Yokohama (Japan). Passengers were briefed about the planned rebellion and courtesy Kartar Singh Sarabha, they were also handed 200 revolvers and 2000 rounds of ammunition. After reaching India, Kartar Singh increased his activity and visited Bengal to secure weapons and made contact with revolutionaries like Vishnu Ganesh Pingley with whom he visited military cantonments in UP, Punjab and Rawalpindi with a view to incite soldiers to revolt. After arrest, Kartar was asked to leave the country and proceed to Kabul. But he did not want to leave the battlefield and finally was arrested on 2nd. March 1915. Many of the Ghadarites paid a heavy price – some were sent to gallows, others were imprisoned for life and some were placed under custody. In all, 9 cases were tried in Lahore (then it was part of the undivided Punjab of British Raj). This is known as First Lahore Conspiracy Case. It was tried by a special tribunal constituted under Defence of India Act, 1915, and seven Indians were hanged till death. These were all Ghadarites and included 19-year-old Kartar Singh Sarabha and 23-year-old Vishnu Govind Pingley.[91] Kartar Singh Sarabha was one of the key architects of the Ghadar Party and a close associate of Lala Hardayal.

Revolutionary Kartar Singh, the great devotee of Bellona, was not even twenty years old when he sacrificed himself on the altar of the goddess of freedom. He appeared like a storm from somewhere, ignited the flame of revolution and tried to awaken the sleeping Bellona. He blazed the holy *yajna* of revolution and became himself an offering for the same. Who was he? From what world did he suddenly appear? And where did he go?

"We were awestruck. Such courage, self-confidence, and dedication are rarely found. Revolution lived in his veins. There was only one aim of his life, only one desire, only one hope - all that held meaning in his life was revolution."[92]

These innocent sacrifices, perhaps, laid a solid foundation and an inspiration for coming generations of revolutionaries like Bhagat Singh, Chandrashekhar Azad and Rajguru.

In Singapore around 37 Ghadar supporters were executed and 41 transported for life, and in the conspiracy trials, around 45 Ghadar leaders were sentenced to death and around 200 were imprisoned.[93]

British Intel noted about Ghadar:

> *"The word Ghadar means mutiny…it is aimed at bringing about a revolution in India in order to secure liberation from British Control. The headquarter of the Ghadar Party was established in San Francisco and the Party published its own paper known as the Ghadar, and founded an institution known as the Jugantar Ashram, the object of the institution being to instill patriotic feelings in young Indians and train them for a uprising in India."*[94]
>
> *"The Ghadar, or Mutiny, derived its origin from the Pacific Coast of America, its centre being at San Francisco. It was stated that the Jugantar Ashram had been founded in San Francisco, and that in this institution books would be compiled, young preachers trained, and preparations for a rising would be taken in hand. It was violently anti-British in nature, playing on every passion that it could possibly excite…and urging all Indians to go to India with*

> *the express intention of committing murders, causing revolution and expelling the British Government by any means."*[95]

Ghadar movement was intense. But the records show that armed rebellion was planned at a time when Britain was engaged in First World War and in India, Mahatma Gandhi and Indian National Congress were in sympathy with the British cause of war. Prayers were performed in Gurudwaras, temples and mosques for the victory of the British. Many texts note and attribute failure of Ghadar movement to poor sense of security, not taking steps to avoid information leak and failure to grasp choices of the Indian people. But the architects of *Ghadar* were not war strategist; they were nationalist editors, who did their journalistic duty with utmost dedication and sacrificed their life. Strategic infiltration by British intelligence was something they were not trained to deal with.

It was during the gradual uncovering of the Lahore conspiracy case that led to another conspiracy known as Hindu–German conspiracy. Though from name it seems it was a conspiracy between India and Germany against the imperialist rule of India, but it had many fine layers like members of Irish Republican Army, many intellectuals in US, officials from German embassy were part this conspiracy. It was also a well-conceived plan that involved the secret shipment of arms and rebels from the US West Coast across the Pacific Ocean to India where revolution-ready Indians were waiting. One Sukumar Chatterjee was arrested by British intelligence in Bangkok in June 1917. He broke under pressure and admitted receiving money from a real estate agent in Chicago.

"During World War I, Indian nationalists used Great Britain's preoccupation with the European war to attempt to foment revolution in India to overthrow British rule. Their activities were aided politically and financially by the German Government. Indian nationalists in the United States were active in the independence movement effort through fund-raising, arms buying, and propagandizing through the *Ghadar* newspaper published from San Francisco.

The Justice Department and US Attorney records documented activities of the Indian Independence Movement in the US from 1908 onwards. The US government's primary concern was the prosecution of these nationalists in the "Hindu Conspiracy Case" (as it was called in the press and Department of Justice correspondence) for violations of the Espionage Act. It focused on two major incidents. The first was related to (alleged) funding of nationalist activists by the German government with which arms were procured for shipment to Indian rebels. In the second incident, several Indians (some of whom were US. citizens) and others were arrested for attempted fraud involved in soliciting funds and calling themselves representatives of the "Nationalist Government" of India. In the spring of 1918, the 'Hindu Conspiracy Case' trial was held in San Francisco, at which 29 people were convicted in indictments arising from the arms shipment. Indictments arising from the fraud case were dismissed."

The British Government in India tried its best to get the cases transferred to India, but it wasn't accepted by the US Government.

The second Lahore conspiracy case was about the trial in which Bhagat Singh, Sukhdeo Thapar and Shivram Rajguru, some of the most revered figures of the Indian freedom struggle, were served with capital punishment. They were hanged on March 23, 1931 in Punjab's Hussainawala (now in Pakistan).

On December 17, 1927 Bhagat Singh and Shivram Rajguru shot and killed Asst. Supdt. of Police John Saunders. They were supported in the act by their compatriots Sukhdeo Thapar and Chandra Shekhar Azad (though their original target was Supdt. of Police James Scott who ordered his men to lathi charge protesters, leading to the death of popular leader Lala Lajpat Rai). The case was heard by a special tribunal set up on the directive of Viceroy's Lord Irwin on May 1, 1930. The tribunal had the power to proceed without the presence of accused and was all the way a one-sided trial that hardly adhered to normal legal guidelines. The tribunal delivered its 300-page judgement on October 7, 1930. It declared that irrefutable evidence has been presented confirming the involvement of Bhagat Singh, Sukhdeo Thapar and Shivram Rajguru in Saunders's murder. They were sentenced to be hanged till death. Soon after sentencing, the police raided Hindustan Republican Army Association (HRAA), bomb factories in Lahore and arrested several prominent revolutionaries.

Three individuals, Hansraj Vohra*, Jai Gopal and Phanindra Nath Ghosh, turned approvers of the Government, which lead to total 21 arrests. Further record suggests that on recommendation of the then Viceroy, Vohra was sponsored by the Punjab Government to study in the London School of Economics (LSE). After a Masters in Political Science, he studied journalism in London University. He returned to Lahore and worked as a journalist for *Civil and Military Gazette,* Lahore till 1948. Some available records suggest that in 1958, he went to Washington and after sometime, became the Washington correspondent of *The Times of India.*

In the beginning, the copies of the *Ghadar* were concealed in parcels of foreign cloth sent to Delhi. It was also planned to smuggle a printing press into India for this purpose. But then the war broke out and it became almost impossible to import printing machinery from abroad. Lala Hardayal was arrested in America and deported to India. One of his followers Pt. Ramchandra started publishing *Hindustan Ghadar* in English. With the US joining the war, the Ghadar party workers were arrested by the American Government.[96] When the trial was on, one of the rivals and a fellow defendant Ram Singh managed to obtain a gun

---

* *While going through various references, one can find article/s claiming the innocence of Vohra. Readers can form their own opinion based on various references available in the public domain.*

and shot Pt. Ramchandra dead. The death of Ramchandra led to the closure of this paper. [97]

Monitoring of Indian newspapers: Rise of nationalism was quite a concern for British, and newspapers and journals published from India were closely monitored in London. The following are extracts taken from the report that has been preserved in micro-film and forms the part of Indian newspaper Reports, c1868–1942 in the British Library, London. It is clear from the exhaustive report that nationalism got its momentum after 1857, and mostly vernacular press was in the forefront of the movement.

The following are excerpts are from the reports for 1901:

The Indian Appeal (Benares) of the10th May says: - Many of us will agree with the Viceroy when he told the Muhammedans, that the twentieth century was certain, whatever else it might bring forth, to be a century of great intellectual activity, of far reaching scientific discovery, and of probable unparalleled invention. That is all very grand. But what part are the Indians going to play in this intellectual arena….?"

The Roznamcha-i-Qaisari (Allahabad), of the 15th September, complains that it would seem that a European gentleman has kicked a native to death near the Allahabad Railway Station. It is a pity that the life of a native is considered to be of no more value than that of a pariah dog. In what a helpless condition the natives are! May God have mercy on them!. "

The following are from the reports for 1910:

> *"…the editor of the Karmayogi (Allahabad) writes: There are many obstacles in the way of Indian nationalists…. Indians, should however never lose courage, for, no nation was created to occupy forever a subordinate position in this universe. Even those that are ruled over by foreigners today have a right to govern and manage their own affairs themselves…. The editor reminds*

> *his readers that numerous hardships and sufferings will have to be borne and manifold virtues cultivated before India can rise higher in the state of nations....*"

The following is from the reports for 1916:

The *Prem* (Brindaban, Muttra-Mathura, apparently) of the 26th July publishes a poem by Judh Singh Varma deploring the degraded condition of Indians as represented by their abject poverty, starvation, sectarian strives and mutual animosities, the decay of their trade and industry, in the prevalence of famine and disease and in their social degeneration. They have already been reduced to helplessness by the imposition of taxes. He exorts them to shake off indolence, to spread education in the country, to be united for mutual service, to give up evil social customs to cultivate physical culture and to be self-respecting and self-confident. They should take to trade and industry. They should not hanker after service, but seek independence..."

The extracts below are from the reports for January 1928 regarding the Muslim League and the Liberal Federation:

> *"Very few papers have so far commented on the proceedings of the Muslim League. The Leader wrote: - The split in the Muslim League will be regretted by those who attach greater importance to communal than national unity.... The Indian Daily Telegraph wrote:- In spite of the great shortcomings which were the outcome of the mischievous anti-national activities of the Shaffian clique, the Calcutta session of the All-Indian Muslim League was a great success....*"

The *Leader* wrote: - The address delivered by Sir Tej Bahadur Sapru as President of the National Liberal Federation of India at Bombay is a master-piece. The whole of the address will be read by our countrymen not only with satisfaction but with pride. It ought to be read by Englishmen with a sense of deep humiliation. But people in whom there is no humility cannot easily be shamed into a confession of wrong-doing...."

The following is from the reports for 1936:

> *"Muslim papers condemn the socialistic & revolutionary program advocated by Mr. Nehru and regard it as being calculated to lead to anarchy and a bloody civil war.... Some Muslim papers deplored the paucity of Muslims in the Congress and advised them to join it provided it abandons its anti-Muslim attitude and socialistic policy.... The daily Pratap regards Pt. Nehru's address as a reflection of his career and says that every word of it bears the stamp of sincerity and honesty...."*

After the First World War the Congress Party was taken over by socialists like Jawaharlal Nehru and others. Later, it became associated with Mahatma Gandhi, who, although never a member of the party, became its spiritual leader. Under Gandhi's influence, the party became the true representative of the people by working against caste differences, untouchability, poverty, and religious and ethnic discrimination. In the 1930's there was a series of conferences in London where the making of a new constitution in India was discussed, finally taking the form of the 1935 Government of India Act.

See Appendix I for a detailed report.

Role of Gandhi in the Development of Journalismin India

3

Gandhi is one the most written about persona in the history of humanity. Every aspect of his work and life has been covered by eminent historians and sociologists from around the world. He made non-violence and peaceful agitation the most effective weapon to deal with the violent, tyrant and repressive colonial regime in India. His firm belief in non- violence as the most effective tool has been vastly criticized, but use of any other tool to make India free wouldn't have come without a heavier price. He practiced what he preached in all its entirety and this led to a situation wherein his every word was religiously followed. To be a wonderful leader one has to be a communicator *extraordinaire*. Gandhi had this ability right from the beginning. He was more a written communicator than an orator, and journalism came naturally to him. Ramchandra Guha in his book points out, "In his school examination the young Mohandas had obtained a mere 44.5 per cent in English. But his residence in London, wide reading and diligent practice made him a decent practitioner of written English by the time he turned 30."[1] The Chief Editor of the *Collected Works of Mahatma Gandhi,* Krishnaswami Swaminathan, hailed the transparent simplicity of his literary style. Gandhi's prose, remarked Swaminathan, "is a natural expression of his democratic temper. There is no conscious ornamentation, no obtrusive truck of style calling attention to itself. The Style is blend of the modern manner of an individual sharing his ideas and experiences with his readers, and the impersonal manner of Indian tradition in which the thought is more important than the person expounding it. The sense of equality with common man is the mark of Gandhi's style and his teaching. To feel and appreciate this essence of Gandhi, the man, in his writings and speeches, is the best education for a true democracy."[2]

YOUNG INDIA.

PUBLISHED EVERY WEDNESDAY AND SATURDAY.

BOMBAY, SATURDAY, MAY 10, 1919.

Pragjee Soorjee & Co.

DEALERS IN

ANILINE AND ALIZARINE DYES

SULPHUR COLOURS

DIRECT COLOURS

BASIC COLOURS.

PRAGJEE SOORJEE & CO.

Chartered Bank Building, Esplanade Road, Fort,

BOMBAY.

GODREJ & BOYCE

SAFE MAKERS

EMPIRE AUTOMOBILES.

HARVEY FROST

Motor Accessories Supply COMPANY

AN EMPORIUM OF

Surajmal Lalubhai & Co.

DIAMOND MERCHANTS

The Indian Mercantile Insurance Co., Ld.

For

Marble

English Flooring Tiles

Broken Mosaic Tiles

Asbestos Cement

Sheets and Stencil-ings

RAVAL & Co.

USE THIS WONDERFUL MACHINE FOR ICECREAM

SETHNA & CO.

Young India: courtesy: Page URL:https://commons.wikimedia.org/wiki/File:Young_India.png, File URL:https://upload.wikimedia.org/wikipedia/commons/6/63/Young_India.png

As Sunil Khilnani observes, "like Jawaharlal Nehru, Gandhi wrote English well enough to have made, if he had so wished, a living through journalism. One reason he wrote the foreign tongue as well as was that he 'ruthlessly excised' from his own work the exaggeration and melodrama so characteristic of Indian writing."[3] Thus, Gandhi's prose came to be marked, in Khilnani's words, by the "clarity of its argumentation and directness of its expression". However, to limit these qualities of his prose to his English writings only would be a bit myopic and accepting a half-truth. He was equally direct in his writing in Gujarati and Hindi. That's why *Indian Opinion* – though started in English – was soon followed by editions in Hindi, Tamil and Gujarati.[4] He, perhaps, firmly believed that rulers and the ruled one in India could not be addressed by a single language alone.[4] English was the language of rulers, but he was religiously followed by thousands among Indian diasporas living in Johannesburg. At one hand, he wanted to represent the grievances of South African Indians to the rulers and on the other hand, he wanted to keep Indian diasporas informed about his activities. And the best and more direct way of informing them was to inform them in their own language, i.e., Hindi, Tamil and Gujarati. So, he wasn't doing his duty as a journalist alone but also carried out the work that was naturally expected from a leader and statesman. In a way, he was more than a journalist right from the beginning, and his successes in both these fields only got better with time.

It is clear that Gandhi had an urge to express himself right from the beginning – a quality so much needed to become a writer and journalist. He first came across a publication when he was studying law in London. The publication was *The Vegetarian,* a magazine which was published by the Vegetarian Society to promote vegetarianism among its members. Gandhi, himself a vegetarian, wrote a piece on the Indian aspect of vegetarianism and was published under the title 'Indian Vegetarian' in its issue dated on February 7, 1891.[5] It is considered to be the first published work by Gandhi in any publication. Gandhi must have written the piece to express his views on the vegetarian way of life, but having his name appeared in print was no less an enticement. He contributed 9 articles for the magazine and, as they say, "rest is history". Apart from being a national leader and social reformer, Gandhi was a great communicator. These qualities were so closely interwoven in him that it was difficult to separate one from another. More than anyone else, he recognized that communication was the most effective tool to shape opinion and mobilize popular support. He was successful because he had a latent skill in communication that surfaced in South Africa where he had gone initially to practice as a lawyer. The practice of communication started by him in South Africa gave him the clue to rally millions of his countrymen when he returned to India. In South Africa, where he chose to practice law, he was thrown in to the vortex of politics that shaped his career as a journalist, politician and social reformer.[6] In October 1899, when the Boer War broke out, Gandhi – along with Indian volunteers – jumped to serve the sick and wounded.

Three Boer Wars were fought from October 11, 1899 until May 31, 1902 between the United Kingdom and the South African Republic (Transvaal Republic) and Orange Free State. The British war effort was supported by troops from several regions in the British Empire, including Southern Africa, the Australian colonies, Canada, India and New Zealand. The war ended in victory for Britain and the annexation of both republics. Both would eventually be incorporated into the Union of South Africa in 1910.

Gandhi was associated with six journals, for two of which he was the editor. His first paper *Indian Opinion* was started in South Africa. In order to ventilate the grievances of Indians and mobilize public opinion in their favor, Gandhi started writing and giving interviews to newspapers. He focused on open letters and Letters to Editor, but soon realized that occasional writings and the hospitality of newspapers were inadequate for the political campaign he had launched. He needed a mouthpiece to reach out to the people. So, in June 1903 he launched *Indian Opinion*. It served the purpose of a weekly newsletter, which disseminated the news of the week among the Indian community. It became an important instrument of education. Through the columns of the newspaper, Gandhi tried to educate readers about sanitation, self-discipline and good citizenship. "We are far from assuming that the Indians here are free from all the faults that are ascribed to them. Wherever we find them to be at fault, we will unhesitatingly point it out and suggest means for their removal."[6] Gandhi started *Indian Opinion* for three basic purposes:

- to give a voice to the feeling of the Indian community in South Africa
- to raise the voice of dissent – to represent the grievances of Indian diasporas to the rulers
- to unite the diverse elements among diasporas.

As the journal wrote, "we are not, and ought not to be, Tamil or Calcutta man, Mohammedans or Hindus, Brahmans or Baniyas, but simply and solely British Indians, and as such we must sink or swim together."[7]

It was the democratic temper of Gandhi which prompted him to even turn inwards when throwing a flashlight on other corners of the society. [*This is significant because, in the long journey, the Indian press, perhaps, did away with the practice of looking inwards. The point has been further elaborated in Chapter VI- Epilogue*]

How important the journal was to Gandhi is seen from his own statement in his biography *My Experiments with Truth*: "*Indian Opinion*... was a part of my life. Week after week I poured out my soul in its columns and expounded the principles and practice of satyagraha, as I understood it. During 10 years, that is until 1914, excepting the intervals of my enforced rest in prison there was hardly an issue of *Indian Opinion* without an article from me. I cannot recall a word in these articles set down without thought or deliberation or word of conscious exaggeration, or anything merely to please. Indeed, the journal became for me training in self- restraint and for friends a medium through which to keep in touch with my thoughts."

He had clarity about using Indian languages. While editing *Navjeevan,* he wrote, "The editing of *Navajivan* has been a kind of a revelation to me. Whilst *Young India* has little more than 1200 subscribers, *Navjeevan* has 12,000. The number would leap to 20,000, if the printer is able to print that number. It shows that a vernacular newspaper is a felt want."

After Gandhi's departure from South Africa in 1914, *Indian Opinion* was edited by his son Mani Lal Gandhi.

The advent of Gandhi in to Indian politics ushered a new era in journalism. The press was also introduced to new ideas and thoughts. Gandhi's belief in non-violence and peaceful resistance was like fresh and positive answers to many questions that Indians were facing. Gandhi firmly believed in what he did and he did what he firmly believed in. That's why every word of his was taken seriously. Journalism in that era took a separate path from prevalent extremist ideologies under the influence of Gandhi and changed the tone and temper of Indian journalism. Gandhi's idea of Satyagraha, civil disobedience and non-violence touched everyone's heart, and newspapers at that time whole heartedly supported these ideas. *Matwala,* in its editorial, published on March 31, 1934 said, "If you wish to be independent and want Swaraj, immediately start obeying (your leader) Gandhi's orders in its entirety."[8]

So huge was the impact of Gandhi that newspapers and journals did everything to spread his message in far-flung areas. *Aaj* from Varanasi fully dedicated itself to Gandhi's ideas, and inspired the publication of other dailies like *Vartman* from Kanpur (November 23, 1920). *Vartman* also fully dedicated itself to the cause of the nationalist movement and ideals of Gandhi. In its issue dated January 26, 1921 *Vartman* published an appeal to the youth of the country in which it said, "If you are a true son (of your motherland), be like Prahālād and free me from all my miseries and pain by peaceful and moralistic means." This was evident that the concept of an appeal for peaceful morality was clearly an influence of Gandhi.[9] *Pratap* in its issue dated August 22, 1921 under title *Swaraj Lena* (having self-rule) wrote, "Let (them) pass Rowlatt acts in thousands; let (them) repeat Jalianwala massacre millions of times and let (them even) lock our tongues – but finally we will have swaraj."

The eminent journalist and freedom fighter Sailen Chatterjee, who covered Mahatma Gandhi, his actions and programs for a number of years, said in an article:

> *"I joined journalism in 1942. Reporting Mahatma Gandhi and my tours with him were the best and most memorable period of my journalistic career. Gandhiji himself was a journalist. During my tours with him, he often told me how he worked day and night to produce his journal Indian Opinion in Natal, South Africa. He described Indian Opinion as the most useful weapon in his struggle in South Africa. He always stressed the importance of newspapers in educating people. Gandhiji always believed and emphasized that the sole aim of journalism should be service, service of the people and the country."*[10]

Gandhi wrote his autobiography in Gujarati *Satin Paryogo Athwa Aatmakatha.* This was translated by Mahadeo Desai into English. The Gujarati version was serialized weekly in *Navjeevan* and its English translation was published in *Young India*. Gandhi started *Young India* weekly in 1919 to promote his views on politics and other topics. Fourteen years later, the paper changed its name to *Harijan*. In *Young India,* Gandhi once gave a glimpse of the exacting code of ethics he had set up for himself, "To be true to my faith, I may not write in anger or malice. I may not write idly. I may not write merely to excite passion.

The reader can have no idea of the restraint I have to exercise from week to week in the choice of topics and my vocabulary. It is training for me. It enables me to peep into myself and to make discoveries of my weaknesses. Often my vanity dictates a smart expression or my anger a harsh adjective. It is a terrible ordeal but a fine exercise to remove these weeds."[11]

Gandhi had been frequently writing on various aspects of journalism as a profession too. To him editorial independence, adherence to truth and self-restraints were the three overriding considerations for journalism. In his message for the editor of the newspaper *The Independence* on 30 January 1919, he wrote, "In wishing you success in your new enterprise, I would like to say how I hope your writings would be worthy of the title you have chosen for your journal; and may I further hope that with independence you will add an equal measure of self-restraint and the strictest adherence to truth. Too often in our journals as in others do we get fiction instead of fact and declamation in place of sober reasoning. You would make *The Independence* a power in the land and a means of education for the people by avoiding the errors I have drawn attention to."[12]

On receiving advertisement support for running a newspaper, Mahatma Gandhi wrote, "It is now an established practice with newspapers to depend for revenues mainly from advertisements rather than on subscriptions. The result has been appalling or shocking that has led newspapers to live and survive in contradictions. The very newspaper which writes against the iniquity of wine publishes advertisements in praise of wines in the same issue, newspapers at one hand carry write-ups on harmful aspect of tobacco and on the other they also tell their readers from where to buy it. Or we shall find the same issue of a paper carrying a long advertisement for a certain play and denouncing that play as well. Medical advertisements are the largest source of revenue though they have done harm, and are still doing immense harm to the people. These medical advertisements almost wholly eclipsed the services rendered by the newspapers and forfeit the very purpose of it. I have been eyewitness to the harm done by them. Many people are lured into buying harmful medicines.[13] Many of these promote immorality. Such advertisements find a place even in papers that are run to further the cause of religion. This practice has come entirely from the West. No matter at what cost or effort, we must put an end to this undesirable practice or at least reform. It is the duty of every newspaper to exercise some restraint in the matter of advertisements."[14]

History of newspapers show that instead of trying to get rid of unscrupulous advertisements, with time, newspapers became hugely dependent on it, and a time came when such advertisements became the driving force in newspaper business. Such dependence certainly led to a situation where newspapers were not only eroded of its fundamental duty of informing and educating its readers but it also became a refuge for such advertisements and hugely depended on the money made from it. One can look at the Mahatma's journalistic forays in either of two ways: as the moralist who took to journalism or as the journalist who undertook a moral crusade. That he was a crusader par excellence is unquestionable. He crusaded for morality in politics and in public life. He left his readers – especially all Congressmen – in no doubt as to what he expected of them.[15]

Today, when there is widespread concern over the growing influence of market forces on media, and regret over journalism being no longer a social service, Gandhi's views on values of journalism bring to bear on the profession of journalism the force of ethics and morality. In this context, he had said, "It is often observed that newspapers published any matter that they have, just to fill in space. The reason is that most newspapers have their eyes on profits. There are newspapers in the West which are so full of trash that it will be a sin even to touch them. At times, they produce bitterness and strife even between different families and communities."

There never was an no editor like him before and there never will be another like him. The times, of course, made the man. But the man contributed to his times in many wondrous ways.[16]

According to Chalapathi Raju, Gandhi was probably the greatest journalist of all time, and the weeklies he ran and edited were probably the greatest weeklies the world has known. He published no advertisements, and at the same time he did not want his newspapers to run at a loss. Gandhi looked upon journalism as a means to serve the people. He said in his autobiography, "The sole aim of journalism should be service. The newspaper is a great power, but just as an unchained torrent of water submerges whole countryside and devastates crops, even so an uncontrolled pen serves but to destroy. If the control is from outside, it proves more poisonous than want of control. It can be profitable only when exercised from within."[17] If this line of reasoning is correct, how many journals of the world would stand the test? But who would stop those that are useless? And who should be the judge? The useful and the useless must, like good and evil, go on together, and a reader must make his choice.

Role of the Media with Special Reference to Newspapers Published from 1780–1980

4

James Augustus Hicky started the first newspaper *Bengal Gazette or The Original Calcutta General Advertiser* in Calcutta on January 29, 1780. The paper had to close down in March, 1782. Thereafter, several newspapers came into existence in Bombay, Calcutta and Madras, but they all had a short life. A number of legal restrictions were imposed on the press by the British rulers. On July 2, 1840 the *Bengal Gazette* was published. From there up to the turn of 20th century we see a comparatively stable period in Indian journalism where it experimented with new ideas to quench the intellectual thirst of its readers. The period also saw some extraordinary contributions from some other English journalists, which helped in bringing even scientific interest within the purview of journalism. For sometime past, the Asiatic Society (founded in 1784 by Sir William Johns) had been publishing papers related to Zoology, Botany, Geology, Chemistry, Physics, Anthropology, Meteorology and Medicine. *The Journal of Asiatic Society* incorporated the publication named *Gleanings in Science*, three volumes of which were published during 1829–1831.

Subsequently, the *Indian Review* and *Journal of Foreign Science*, which were published in 8 volumes between 1834–1847, were also incorporated in the *Journal of the Asiatic Society*. Kishori Mohan Ganguli published *HaliShahar Patrika*, which translated *Mahabharata* in to English. He was one of the outstanding journalists of the time.

By 1839, Calcutta had 26 Anglo-Indian newspapers, including six dailies and total number of subscribers to English newspapers in Calcutta was calculated to be 2205. The War of Independence in 1857 saw the freedom of the press curtailed drastically. After the end of the mutiny, the control over India changed hands from the East India Company to the Crown of England. Many newspapers in English and Indian languages came into existence soon after. Journalism in those times not only reflected public sentiments but also shaped the public opinion. Press became as sacrosanct as Geeta, Quran or Bible. In course of time, a large number of political leaders, thinkers and journalists, such as Mahatma Gandhi, Jawaharlal Nehru, Motilal Ghosh, Maulana Abul Kalam Azad, came to be associated with the press. Most of the eminent journalists were freedom fighters and likewise many of the freedom fighters were journalists. The press received a remarkable support from the people and despite the numerous ruthless laws, it continued to grow. 1857 was a turning point in more ways than one. With couple of effective newspapers and a potent system of intelligence in place, British administration was taken aback by the revolt of 1857. None of these systems could sense a revolt of such a high order. Indian press was a natural victim and provided a veil behind which British could hide their failure. So, many forms of restriction were imposed on newspapers. But at home, the British East India Company also came under huge criticism. Before that, how the Company was conducting its affairs in India and at home furnishes some stark details.

According to an article in International weekly *Economist*, the East India Company, as a trader, did many things that shows how clever it was in dealing with and how it gave bribes and it did not hesitate to bully when its purpose was not served.

"The East India Company foreshadows the modern world in all sorts of striking ways. It was the first company to offer limited liability to its shareholders. It laid the foundation of British Empire, it spawned company man. The company created a powerful East India lobby in parliament, caucus of MPs who had directly or indirectly profited from its business, and who constituted, in Edmund Burkey's opinion, one of the most lineated and formidable force in British politics. It also made regular gifts to (the court) — 'All who could help or hurt at court,' wrote Lord Macaulay, 'Ministers, mistresses, priests were kept in good humour by presents of shawls and silks, bird's nest and attar of roses......of diamonds and bags of guineas. It also made timely gifts to the treasury whenever the state faced bankruptcy. In short it acted as what George Dempster, a stakeholder called a — great money engine of the state.' The Company was just adapting at playing politics abroad. It distributed bribe liberally to the merchants, offered to provide an English virgin for the sultan of Achin's harem, for example, before James I intervened. And where it could not bribe it bullied, using soldiers paid for by Indian taxes to duff up recalcitrant rulers. Indeed, its most valuable skill-core competence in the phrase beloved of management theorists, was less its ability to arrange long-distance voyages to India and beyond, than its ability to manage the politicians back home."[4]

The company's growing interest in politics infuriated its mighty army of critics still further. How could it justify having a monopoly of trade as well as right to tax the citizens of India? And how could a commercial organization justify ruling 90 million Indians, controlling 70 million acres (2,43,000 square kilometres) of land, issuing its own coins, compete with the Crown's court and supporting an army of 2,00,000? Adam Smith denounced the company as a bloodstained monopoly: burdensome, useless and responsible for grotesque massacre of Bengal.

Anti-Company opinion hardened further in 1770 when a famine wiped out a third of the population of Bengal, reducing local productivity, depressing the company's business and eventually forcing it to go cap in hand to the British Government to avoid bankruptcy.[5] (Warren Hastings's 1772 report estimated that a third of the population in the affected region starved to death.)

After 1757, when Sir Robert Clive won the battle of Plassey (the battle helped the Company seize control of Bengal. Over the next hundred years, they seized control of the entire Indian subcontinent and Myanmar, and briefly Afghanistan), and delivered the Government of Bengal to the Company. Slowly but surely, revenue replaced commerce as the Company's first concern. Tax rolls replaced business ledgers. Arsenals replaced warehouses. C N Parkinson summarized how far it had strayed, by 1800, from its commercial purpose, "How was the East India Company controlled? By the Government. What was its object? To collect taxes. How was its object attained? By means of standing army. Who were its employees? Soldiers, mostly, the rest, civil servants."

In 1858, one year after the Indian mutiny, many things happened in quick succession which left the Company stunned. The Government took over the administrative duties in India. The Company's headquarter in London, East India House, was demolished in 1862. It paid the last dividend in 1873 and was finally put out of its misery in 1874. Thus, an organization that had been given life by the State was eventually extinguished by it.(Queen Victoria, of kindom of Geart Britain, and Ireland adopted additional title of The Empress of India in 1876.)

The failure of the British to anticipate the revolt of 1857 was the turning point in the history of development of newspapers in the country. To avoid such replication in the future, the administration unleashed a number of measures that were used as gagging instruments for the press. But this near successful War of Independence prompted Indian people to make their voices heard more aggressively that eventually lead to the proliferation of language press. Language press was more vocal and direct in their attack on the tyranny of British rule and helped a long way in creating an ambiance where slavery of any kind, body or mind was depicted as detrimental to the fulfillment of hope and aspiration of the people of the nation.[6]

As Calcutta was the capital of India till 1912, initially this served as an epicenter for journalistic endeavors, and not only the English but

Bengali, Hindi, Persian and Urdu newspapers first appeared from this city. From here, these papers could easily avail of the official patronage in the shape of court notices and advertisements along with other benefits of a metropolis, including printing press, machinery and its servicing.[7] Initially Hicky and Buckingham and some other European journalists laid the foundation of what came to be known as Anglo-Indian press. The term "Anglo-Indian" is still a popular terminology in other spheres of social life as well. The Bengal press, for almost a century, remained representative of Indian press.

Indian English journalism would always remain indebted to a couple of English journalists for not only laying the foundation of the profession here but instilling a fight-unto-finish instinct in to journalism that is the very core of the profession.

James Augustus Hicky, Silk Buckingham and Robert Knight are uniquely positioned in the history and development of English journalism in India. All of these three fought against the administration, rarely compromised, and accepted harshest of punishments, risking their professional and personal lives. James Augustus Hicky was viewed by some as talented and arrogant,[8] but one should not forget that being himself an Englishman, he never shied away from criticizing the administration. His silencing by the authorities paved the way for proliferation of many pro-Government newspapers, and very soon a time came when newspapers were racing against each other in appeasing the Government.[9] But nonetheless, the legacy of Hicky's fighting spirit became the foundation for the next line of editors to show perseverance of the highest degree till the independence of the country was achieved.

Robert Knight (1825–1892) arrived in Bombay in 1847 at the age of 22. Knight was the son of a bank clerk from a lower-middle-class South London neighbourhood, and his life was a cipher before he benefited from a family friend with a job as the Bombay agent for a London wine merchant in the first of a series of unsuccessful business opportunities.

To make ends meet, Knight wrote articles for local newspapers –a necessity after marrying a customs official's daughter and starting on a family of twelve children. His interest or compulsion turned into a career when he filled in for the vacationing editor of *Bombay Times and Journal of Commerce* in 1857.[10] The paper was established in 1838 and issued its first edition on 3rd November of the same year. (It is this paper which later flourished as *The Times of India*). In the beginning it was a bi-weekly published on Wednesdays and Saturdays under the stewardship of Raibahadur Narayan Dinanath Velkar, a Maharashtrian reformist leader, and contained news from Britain and the world, as well as the Indian subcontinent. J.E. Brennan was its first editor. In 1850, it began to publish daily editions.

Knight, as an editor, wanted to perform and perform better than his Anglo-Indian counterparts. Thus, he was quick to recognize a void to be filled in when the Sepoy Mutiny exploded. Knight straightaway decried the British administration, and instead blamed the violence on the lack of discipline and poor leadership in the army.[11] Unpopular with the Anglo community, Knight's struck a chord with the *Times'* Indian shareholders, and he was quickly made editor permanently. Knight continued to be a critique of the mismanagement of the British Raj, its annexation policies that appropriated native lands and arbitrarily imposed taxes on previously exempt land titles, ridiculous income taxes, and educational systems that disregarded Indian customs and needs. While some accused Knight of sycophancy to his Indian bosses, Hirschman (Knight's biographer) instead sees the moral indignation of one whose own experiences as a social outsider had led to an ingrained sympathy for the disadvantaged and disgust for the duplicities of British rule.[12]

Knight led the *The Times* to national prominence. In 1860, he bought out the Indian shares and merged with the rival *Bombay Standard* while starting India's first news agency (wiring *Times* dispatches to subscribers across the country) and becoming the Indian agent for Reuters news service. In 1861, he changed the name from the *Bombay Times and Standard* to the *The Times of India.* Seven years later, business quarrels led him to sell his shares to his business partners and launch a new venture, a periodical called the *Indian Economist* (1869) that focused on financial news. Other sources indicate Knight's arrival in Calcutta in 1872, where he was offered post of Assistant Secretary in Department of Agriculture of Bengal Government and in this capacity, he edited *The Agriculture Gazette of India.* But he resigned from the government service in 1875, and same year brought the journal *Friend of India* (Hirschman had put it as *Star of India)*, which had been founded by the Missionaries of Serampur in 1818, and transferred it to Calcutta. Knight founded *The Statesman* and later he merged both. For several years, the paper appeared as *Statesman and the Friend of India.*[13] He started this new paper with the help of 24 merchants who took shares in it. Knight had to face some rivalry from other press (actually Knight started the price war by cutting the price of his paper by 1/4th), but Knight was too good for them and before long, he began to exert considerable influence on the Government and press circles in Calcutta.[14] After the death of Knight in 1890, his sons Paul and Robert got control of the paper. [Author's note: Couple of facts stated above are based on Bihar District gazetteer, government of Bihar1971 edited by N.Kumar. Gazeteers have been publications of hallmark authenticity. In N. Kumar's description, the sequence of events that led to the birth of *The Statesman* is more clearly explained and seems more plausible. Kumar was based at Patna at the time of publication of the Gazette and as a Government-assigned editor, he would have easy access to authentic resources required to complete the Gazette. But there is a larger agreement that Knight was the one who edited Bombay *Times of India*, took it to national fame, came to Calcutta and laid the foundation of another great paper *The Statesman*.]

The Times of India – popularly known as *Times* – had frequent change in its ownership until 1892, when Thomas Bennett and Frank Morris Coleman formed a company Bennett Coleman & Co. Ltd. In 1946 the company was sold to Indian sugar magnate R.K. Dalmiya who had to sell the newspaper to his son-in-law Sahu Shanti Prasad Jain. It remains the property of the Jain family and company continues as Bennett Coleman & Co. Ltd.[4] It has graduated to become one of largest media conglomerates in Asia, and its flagship *The Times of India* is now the largest-selling English daily in the world. It also publishes a daily in Hindi *Navbharat Times,* a daily in Marathi *Maharashtra Times* and an economic daily *The Economic Times* – all of these are multi-edition dailies and brand leaders in their own segments. During 1960s and 1970s, *Times* had publications covering every aspect of life, apart from its dailies. It also published land mark weeklies like *Illustrated Weekly of India* (edited by Sean Mandy, A S Raman, the first Indian editor, then Subrata Bannerjee, Khushwant Singh, M V Kamath and Pritish Nandy), *Dharmayug* (Hindi weekly edited by Pt. Satyakam Vidyalankar and Dr. Dharmaveer Bharati), *Sarika* (a monthly edited by Mohan Rakesh and Kamleshwar), *Madhuri* (film fortnightly edited by Arvind Kumar, Vinod Tewari), *Femina* (women's fortnightly initially edited by Vimal Patil), Science Today (a science monthly edited by Surendra Jha), *Filmfare* (edited by B K Karanjia and K Vikram Singh), *Youth Times* (edited by Ms. Anees Jung) *Dinman* (India's first true international news weekly in Hindi edited by Sachchidanand Heeranand Vastyaya Agyeya and Raghubir Sahay), *Parag* (children's weekly edited by Kanhaiya Lal Nandan), *Indrazal Comics* in English, Hindi, Marathi – all these publications were epitomes of journalistic excellence and nurturing ground for many of the Indian talents who carried the legacy of these great publications forward to many other publications as well, and became a star in their own right. All Hindi magazines mentioned above do not exist today but their contribution to Hindi journalism and Hindi language will be remembered for a long time to come.

In English, *Filmfare* and *Femina* do exist today. *Illustrated Weekly of India* was mired in controversy and ceased publication after 130 years of glorious performance. *Times Content* sadly notes about famous Weekly "(it became) a victim of many circumstances including its own success." *Times Content* provides microfilm of back issues for interested customers.) However, all dailies, including *The Times of India,* not only survived but still maintain the foremost position in their language segment.

Throughout the late 20th century, it was home for the best available intellectual editors, journalists, cartoonists, designers and photographers under one roof. It had its own studio in the office where photoshoot for covers of magazines was arranged. These editors not only produced the best magazines (both in terms of content and circulation; during their peak both weeklies, *Illustrated Weekly of India* and *Dharmayug,* crossed circulation of more than 3.50 lac)[15] but ensured that best journalistic standards (both moral and ethical) were also maintained. *Times* ran its own fellowship trainee scheme for journalist and managers in which applicants had to go through a tough selection procedure.

The present day *The Statesman* is a direct descendant of the two newspapers *The Statesman* and *Friends of India,* and not *Statesman* and *Englishman* as suggested in some references. The two newspapers *Indian Daily News* and *Englishman* were direct rivals of the *Statesman.* The *Statesman* was managed by 24 merchants of British Corporate until its ownership was transferred to an Indian company in the mid-1960s. The first Indian editor assigned under this new ownership was Pran Chopra. It is now published simultaneously from Calcutta, New Delhi, Siliguri and Bhubaneshwar, and has an average weekly circulation of 180,000 and the *Sunday Statesman* has a circulation of 2,30,000. "*Statesman* is known for its independent editorial stance, and it is respected for the fairness of its coverage of different point of views. Its audience includes opinion leaders and intellectuals from across Indian Society."[16]

Free Press of India was founded in 1927. The fact that the Reuter and the Associated Press received money from government offices for supply of news, scared the contemporary nationalist movement from reposing confidence in them and consequently, it decided to establish a nationalist news agency, which found expression in the *Free Press of India*. S. Sadanand was initially its Managing Editor. It had correspondents throughout India and was thus able to give wide publicity to nationalist views. In October, 1932, the *Free Press of India* began supply of world services of news. This expansion of activity was undertaken to meet the demands of newspapers which were anxious to subscribe to news service, which would be so comprehensive as to enable them to dispense off with the services of the *Associated Press* and *Reuters**.[17] Accordingly, *Free Press of India* entered into arrangements with the *Exchange Telegraph*, the *Central News* and the *British United Press of London* for the supply of the news service of these agencies. Their services were received in the London office of the *Free Press* where they were processed and then cabled back to India.[18]

A press ordinance was promulgated on May 30, 1930, giving the Government the authority to order the suspension of newspapers. In course of the Civil Disobedience Movement which followed, whenever the Government saw a cause for action, the press ordinance was invoked and a number of nationalist newspapers suspended publication, while others were forfeited of security and some editors were also arrested.

These developments gave a serious blow to this nationalist news agency. With the closing down of newspapers and apprehension that the publication of the *Free Press* telegrams would lead to proceedings against them, the interest of this news agency was put to considerable financial loss. It was a clearing-house of news from nationalist point of view from all parts of India and Burma.[19] In addition, it received news from London dealing with Indian affairs.

Now, though the clearing house existed, the constituents were wanting. Subsequently, the management of this organization, with

---

* *The Reuters and its subsidiaries in India were in receipt of state patronage in return for the supply of news, and so it had to be objective and impersonal in presentation of news. However, that the news agencies must be devoid of "color" is not universally accepted at present.*

the support of leading members of the Indian Mercantile community, launched an English newspaper in Bombay on June 13, 1930 under the name *Free Press Journal.*

The journal led the contemporary journalism in the following direction:

- The paper was published at half an *anna* (1/32 of a ₹) to enable it to reach the readers on a mass scale.
- It featured telegrams of its parent agencies and thus offered the public distinctive reading matters.
- It employed what was called in India a new kind of layout by displaying matter in bold face type and with banner headlines.[20]

Undaunted by adverse situation, the *Free Press of India* enlarged its publishing activity. It sponsored another English daily in Madras, *The Indian Express*, besides a number of newspapers in Marathi and Gujarati. Plans were also being laid for the establishment of the *Free Press* newspapers in all large cities of India. When this project became known to the newspapers in Calcutta, again apprehension was expressed by them as to the propriety of a news service organization publishing a newspaper which would compete with them. Already there had been considerable unprofitable competition among Calcutta nationalist newspapers, and this latest development was one which they felt that they could not regard with equanimity.10 The nationalist newspapers in Bengal were up till now spared competition with the journals of *Free Press* and were supporters of this news agency, but in the present situation, the Calcutta Editor of the *Free Press* Mr. B. Sen Gupta decided to severe his ties with the *Free Press* and set up an independent organization rather than taking the risk of extinction at the hands of the Associated Press of India. His efforts led to the birth of the *United Press of India.*[21]

The *Free Press of India* news agency had collapsed in the middle of 1935. It was much weakened by protracted litigation and was unable to withstand the blow, when the Bombay Government forfeited its securities totaling ₹ 20,000, which had been deposited by the printer and publisher of the *Free Press Journal* under the provisions of the Indian Press (Emergency Powers) Act. *The Indian Express* and *Dhina Mani* of Madras, which were part of the Free Press group of journals, survived, however under different management.[22]

It was this *Indian Express* of S. Sadanand – acquired by Goenka – that went on to become the most sought-after newspaper of the country. Express Tower at Mumbai was a place of hectic activity during days of Emergency. *Indian Express* and *The Statesman* were the most vocal in fighting for the cause of freedom of speech and expression during the darkest hour of press censorship in the country and it did not give up under the severest kinds of pressure tactics of the Government. The group also publishes Hindi daily *Jansatta a*nd Marathi daily *Sakal,* and both are respected dailies in their segments.

Started by Sir George Allen in Allahabad in 1865, *The Pioneer* has the credit of being associated with two Nobel laureates: Rudyard Kipling and Winston Churchill. Kipling served as a sub-editor and reporter. During his stint with the *Pioneer,* he reported from Calcutta and also from Shimla. His reports were as fascinating as his fiction. Churchill served the *Pioneer* in the late 1890s as its War Correspondent during the Tiran campaign of the North-West Frontier of India.[23] In 1872, the editorship passed to A P Sinnett, who had already been editing a newspaper in Hong Kong and had established his reputation as a vigorous writer. Journalistic and literary talent continued to be attracted to *The Pioneer*. The foremost among them was Rudyard Kipling, who worked for the paper as an Assistant Editor from November 1887 to March 1889. Much of his best work was produced while he was in *The Pioneer*. It has had many distinguished persons as its editors. Maitland Park, Sir George Chesney, Clive Ranigan, George Woollcott, Edwing Howard, FW Wilson and Desmond Young were some of the distinguished editors who are still remembered in India as outstanding craftsmen of their trade. In fact, Desmond Young, a full editor at the time when World War II broke out, left behind his deputy in the editor's chair and moved on to where the real action was – Africa, to send in some of the best war reports ever.[24] A by-product was the bestseller *The Desert Fox*, which was later made into a successful movie. Young was also instrumental in planning a new building to house *The Pioneer* in Lucknow. The foundation stone was laid by the then Viceroy of India, the Marquis of Linlithgow, on December 16, 1936. As Dr. Surendra Nath Ghosh, who was the longest serving editor of the paper wrote, celebrating its 125th anniversary, "... a paper that had no rival and covered news from all quarters. Hence the popularity of 48 pages advertising matter which appeared in each issue of *The Pioneer Mail* mirroring the life and lifestyle of bygone era reached far and wide."[25] Kipling's newspaper, the Allahabad *Pioneer* (circulation 5,000) and the Lahore *Civil and Military Gazette* (circulation 4,000) were both virulent mouthpieces of the British Government propaganda. During the First World War, positive publicity was crucial, and the exploits of Indian soldiers were reported in glowing terms.[26] The "Indianisation" process of *The Pioneer* was completed as Dr. Surendra Nath Ghosh took over as the first Indian editor of the paper after Young left in the early 1940s, and went on to become the longest serving editor of the paper. *The Pioneer* was selected as one of the three leading papers in India to represent the World Press in a Tour of the United States Government in 1951.

Today, *The Pioneer*, under Chandan Mitra, comes out from as many as eight cities and is one of the mainstream English language publications to articulate the right-wing perspective, and as some admirers of the paper opine, "thus providing 'the other view' as it were in the dominant Left and Left-of-centre literary culture in the country." However, there are critics of the paper too who lambast the paper for its "ultra" right-wing leaning.[27]

One of the most trusted newspapers of India *The Hindu* is known for its exhaustive coverage of national and international socio-political issues. With the same sincerity and depth, it covers issues related to science and technology, agriculture, industry and environment. It is one of the most techno-savvy presses in India which had a defined role during Indian Independence movement. The most significant aspect of this newspaper is its coverage, which does not look like a duty-free imported shop; rather it carries quality Indian material from a range of diverse fields.

In 1965, *The Times*, London, listed *The Hindu* as one of the world's ten best newspapers. Discussing each of its choices in separate articles, *The Times* wrote: "The Hindu takes the general seriousness to lengths of severity... published in Madras, [it] is the only newspaper which in spite of being published only in a provincial capital is regularly and attentively read in Delhi. It is read not only as a distant and authoritative voice on national affairs but as an expression of the most liberal and least provincial southern attitudes... It's Delhi Bureau gives it outstanding political and economic dispatches and it carries regular and frequent reports from all state capitals, so giving more news from states, other than its own, than most newspapers in India... It might fairly be described as a national voice with a southern accent. The Hindu can claim to be the most respected paper in India."

In 1968, the American Newspaper Publishers' Association awarded *The Hindu* its World Press Achievement Award. An extract from the citation reads: "Throughout nearly a century of its publication *The Hindu* has exerted wide influence not only in Madras but throughout India. Conservative in both tone and appearance, it has wide appeal to the English-speaking segment of the population and wide readership among Government officials and business leaders... *The Hindu* has provided its readers a broad and balanced news coverage, enterprising reporting and a sober and thoughtful comment... [It] has provided its country a model of journalistic excellence... [It] has fought for a greater measure of humanity for India and its people... [and] has not confined itself to a narrow chauvinism. Its correspondents stationed in the major capitals of the world furnish *The Hindu* with world-wide news coverage... For its championing of reason over emotion, for its dedication to principle even in the face of criticism and popular disapproval, for its confidence in the future, it has earned the respect of its community, its country, and the world."

From 1914 to 1947, the freedom struggle continued to gather momentum. All through these years, the Indian press played the role of a guiding light, instilled self confidence in Indian populace and helped them come out from psyche of an indifferent attitude towards governance to active participation, which finally resulted in the independence of the country.

The way the press reacted after Jallianwala Bagh massacre tells all about the power that press had, and it did not shy away from directly criticizing the Government. Jallianwala Bagh massacre happened in 1919. Due to limited communication facilities available at that time, the massacre was not known for many days outside Punjab. General Dyer* ordered his troops to open fire on the people of Amritsar on April 13, 1919, when they were holding a peaceful public meeting at Jallianwala Bagh. The troops fired 1650 rounds of ammunition, which resulted in the death of 379 people and injury to 1137. The then Lt. Governor of Punjab, Sir Michael Francis O'Dwyer, endorsed Dyer's action at Jallianwala Bagh, making it clear that Dyer's order to shoot the crowd was justified. He subsequently administered martial law on April 15, 1919 and backdated it to March 30, 1919.

---

* *After his retirement, Reginald Dyer received a gift of £26,000 sterling from a fund organizsed on his behest by The Morning Post. In the last years of his life, Dyer had several strokes. On July 24, 1927, he passed away at his cottage in Somerset, St Martin's, Long Ashton, near Bristol, after suffering cerebral hemorrhage and arteriosclerosis. Following his death, the reactions in Britain were mixed. The Morning Post hailed him as the "man who saved India", while the 'Westminster Gazette' held the opinion that "No British action, during the whole course of our history in India, has struck a severe blow to Indian faith in British justice than the massacre at Amritsar".*

The British Government suppressed the news. It was known to the public only when Rabindra Nath Tagore returned the title of "Sir" and Shankaran Nair resigned from the Executive Council of Viceroy to protest against the massacre. People of Bihar came to know about it only in August 1919.[28]

On March 13, 1940, in retaliation for the Jallianwala Bagh massacre, Dwyer was assassinated by Indian revolutionary Udham Singh in Caxton Hall, Westminster, London while attending an important meeting of the East India Association and the Central Asian Society (now Royal Society for Asian Affairs). Newspapers openly criticized the heinous act of General Dyer in the strongest of words:

> *"We are now accustomed to the new British ideal that daily expresses itself in Englishman and the Pioneer, and find confirmation in overwhelming votes in the Lords and the Commons. Dyer represents the best mind in Britain, we know what to think of Britain. But we expected some plain speaking from an Indian when Jallianwala Bagh was discussed. General Dyer has shot dead our regard for British Spirit – it lies buried with the bones of Punjabis. The Indian people, bleeding and humiliated, turned to Britain, and what Britain did to India? Britain has treated Dyer as a darling. She has her fingers at us."* [29]

The *Searchlight* published two strong editorials criticizing the British Government for defending General Dyer. On July 25, 1920, it wrote an editorial captioned *The New British Ideal* in condemnation of the English when Lord Finlay justified in the House of Lords – up held by an overwhelming majority – that General Dyer only performed his duty at Jallianwala Bagh. The editorial also condemned Lord Sinha (Satyendra Prasanna Sinha, 1st Baron) for not placing effectively the case of India in the House of Lords. It said –

The House of Lords was held by an overwhelming majority; General Dyer only did his horrible duty at Jallianwala Bagh- that is the meaning of the resolution, as people of India understand it. We have the resolution and we have the figures related to votes. The Indian people do not care to read Lord Finlay's speech.[30]

Indian freedom, simply, would not have been possible without the Indian press.

After India attained independence, the role of the press changed. Jawaharlal Nehru, our first Prime Minister, was a strong champion of the liberty of the press. He, of course, deplored misuse of freedom but, if it came to a question of action, he preferred self-regulation. After gaining independence, many things happened in quick succession. Societal changes that press brought was of paramount importance as it changed the narrative of public discourse world-wide and put media under constant public gaze. Within no time, it came to be known as the "fourth" pillar due to its important role in shaping public opinion. Public opinion is the ultimate in the checks and balance system designed to ensure equal and balanced authorities between the three branches (pillars) of Government, namely: Legislative (who write the law), Executive (who apply the law), and Judiciary (who interpret the law). The media can be seen as an equally important pillar to this balance because its role is to sound the alarm bells in cases of abuse of power, corruption, etc. A further way of keeping the system honest in itself was a huge responsibility. In the West, media started early and matured early but not without some critical observation of a high order.

In any society where newspapers are published, it plays multiple roles. News, articles, and other features carried by the press not only inform but also influence. Public opinion gets created, and Government policies are molded by press reactions. The press also determines the nature of public debates and helps generate discussions on local and national-level issues. There is a direct and visible impact of the press on functioning of the administrative and political systems of a country. Sensitivity to press reports, editorials and comments can stall and also expedite processes of policy formulation. In India, ministers, secretaries and other senior policy advisers to the Central and State Governments are briefed daily with regard to the press reactions, particularly concerning the Minister and the Ministry. Prime Minister's secretariat is known to be making inquiries from ministries and departments whenever adverse or significant press reports appear. Most of the "Short Notice Questions" and other interventions in Parliament and State legislatures are based on information published in national and local newspapers.

Emergency, when democracy was wounded:

Emergency was promulgated in the country on June 25, 1975.

It was a testing time for the grand legacy that the Indian press was bestowed upon during the freedom movement of the country.

Almost all great newspapers were born either during the freedom struggle or they consolidated their position during the freedom struggle. The Indian press, which had shown exemplary courage in fighting the foreign rule, when it came face-to-face with an elected Government of its own people, collapsed under the weight of its rich legacy.

Emergency unmasked the true color, the true face, and the true character of the Indian press that emerged after independence. It was indicative of the fact that during Emergency, the Indian press was put on a trajectory that was not going to dock precisely with the aims and objectives of the freedom of speech and expression, an elements of a much higher orbit.

---

* **Pic:** *This is an iconic photograph of Socialist Leader George Fernandes which became famous during Emergency. Fernandes fought election from jail for Muzaffarpur seat in Bihar and won with a thumping majority. He was Minister of Industries in the Janata Government in 1977.*

Also, it is important to note that an elected Government of its own people resorted to the same coercive tactics and repressive measures that were once used by the autocratic foreign rule. The determination and will to fight simply evaporated into thin air in less than three decades after India became independent.

The proclamation of State of Emergency was signed by the President on June 25, 1975 at 11.45 pm. It was proclaimed in the view of the Bihar movement led by Jayaprakash Narayan which had lengthened its shadow to New Delhi.

The following news from the news agency UNI hit the newspaper offices on June 26, 1975.[1] [Here, the record is taken from *The Searchlight*, a famous daily of Bihar, and its twin publication *Pradeep* as a typical example. These two papers later metamorphosized into *The Hindustan Times* and *Hindustan*.] "The Central Government has issued the following order today under Rule 48 of Defense of India Rules imposing censorship. Whereas the Central Government is of opinion that for the purpose of securing the defense of India and civil defense, the public safety and maintenance of public order, it is necessary to do so.

Now, therefore, in exercise of the powers conferred by the Rule (1) of rule 48 of the Defense of India Rule, 1971, the Central Government hereby makes the following order, namely (1) That no news, comments, rumour or other report, relating to (A) contravention or alleged or purported contravention of any of the provision of part III, Rules 31 and 33 of part IV, Rules 37, 38, 39, 43, 46, 47, 48, 50, 51 and 52 part V, part VIII and part IX of the said Rules including orders made hereunder, or (B) any action taken in relation to such contravention, or (C) any action taken under the provisions of the maintenance of Internal Security Act, 1971 (26 of 1971) shall not be published in any newspaper, periodical or other document unless such news, comments, rumour or other report has been *submitted for scrutiny to an authorised officer and* the *publication, thereof is authorised in writing by such officer.* (2) That no such publication be made except in accordance with such conditions or restrictions as such officer has imposed."

Explanation in this Order: Authorised officer means a Principal Information Officer, Director, Public Relations or Deputy Principal Information Officer in the Press Information Bureau of the Government of India at New Delhi, or a Director of Information or a Director Public Relation of a State Government or Union Territory Administration.

Besides, the press also received a publication guideline from the Press Information Bureau on June 26. The highlights of the guidelines were:

The press is advised to keep the following main points [to be avoided] in view while filing messages, news stories and comments, etc.

a. Any attempt to subvert the functioning of democratidnstitutions.
b. Any attempt to compel members to resign.
c. Anything relating to agitations and violent incidents.
d. Any attempt to incite armed forces and police.
e. Any attempt promoting disintegration and communal passions endangering the unity of the country.
f. Report containing false allegations against leaders.
g. Any attempt at denigrating the institution of the PM.
h. Any attempt endangering law and order to disturb normal functioning.
i. Any attempt to threaten internal stability, production and prospects of economic improvements.

The press suffered during the period not only from illiberal policies of the Government but also from mob violence. A shocking instance was burning down of *The Searchlight* press in Patna in 1974, and the cynical indifference with which the state government treated the affair. It had been warned of the possibility of an attack on the press at least days before, yet nothing was done. After the paper resumed publication with makeshift arrangements, the Government of Bihar delisted *The Searchlight* and its sister publication *Pradeep*, denying advertisements to these papers. Worst of all, it deliberately withheld large sums of money which it owed to the paper for past advertisements.[2] *The Searchlight* and *Pradeep* contested the delisting in Press Council.[3] Finally the delisting order was withdrawn by the Chief Minister Abdul Gafoor on October 27, 1974.

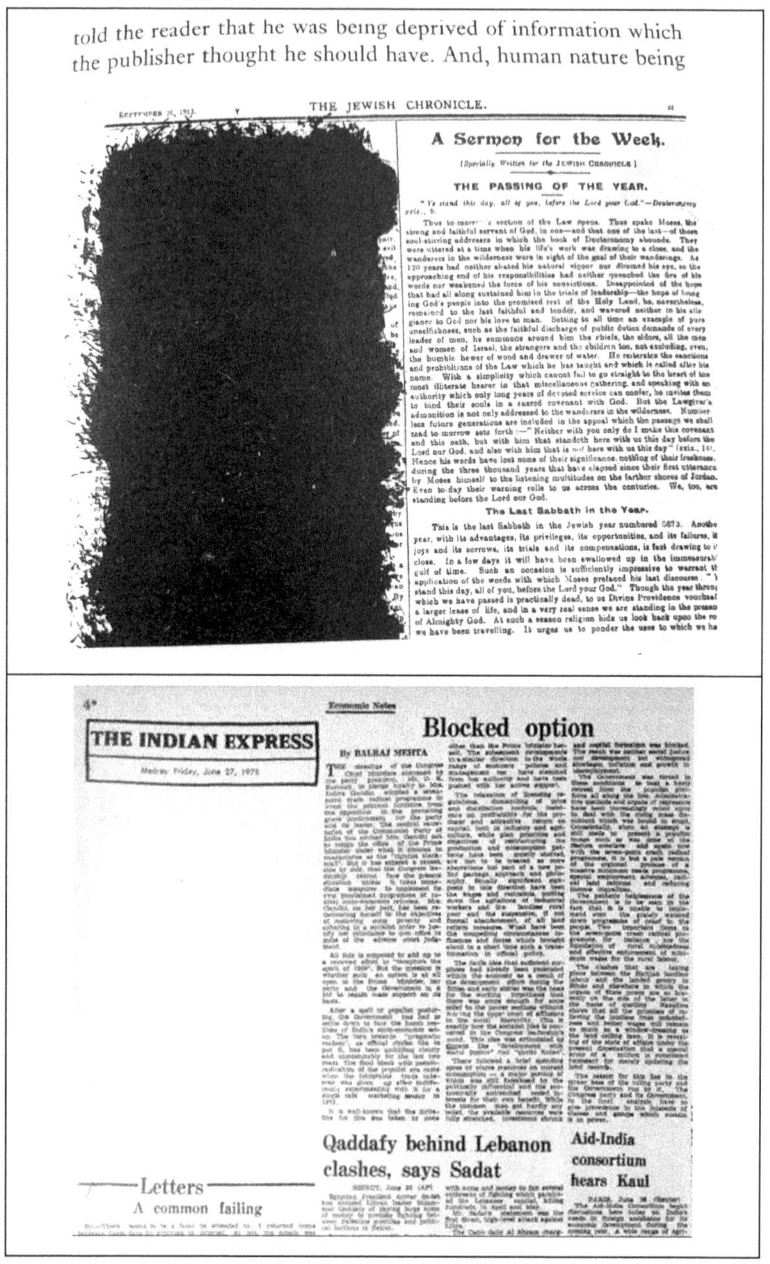

told the reader that he was being deprived of information which the publisher thought he should have. And, human nature being

SEPTEMBER 26, 1913. THE JEWISH CHRONICLE.

A Sermon for the Week.

[Specially Written for the JEWISH CHRONICLE.]

THE PASSING OF THE YEAR.

"Ye stand this day, all of you, before the Lord your God."—Deuteronomy xxix., 9.

Thus to-morrow's section of the Law opens. Thus spake Moses, the strong and faithful servant of God, in one—and that one of the last—of those soul-stirring addresses in which the book of Deuteronomy abounds. They were uttered at a time when his life's work was drawing to a close, and the wanderers in the wilderness were in sight of the goal of their wanderings. As 120 years had neither abated his natural vigour nor dimmed his eye, so the approaching end of his responsibilities had neither quenched the fire of his words nor weakened the force of his convictions. Disappointed of the hope that had all along sustained him in the trials of leadership—the hope of leading God's people into the promised rest of the Holy Land, he, nevertheless, remained to the last faithful and tender, and wavered neither in his allegiance to God nor his love to man. Setting to all time an example of pure unselfishness, such as the faithful discharge of public duties demands of every leader of men, he summons around him the chiefs, the elders, all the men and women of Israel, the strangers and the children too, not excluding, even, the humble hewer of wood and drawer of water. He reiterates the sanctions and prohibitions of the Law which he has taught and which is called after his name. With a simplicity which cannot fail to go straight to the heart of the most illiterate hearer in that miscellaneous gathering, and speaking with an authority which only long years of devoted service can confer, he invites them to bind their souls in a sacred covenant with God. But the Lawgiver's admonition is not only addressed to the wanderers in the wilderness. Numberless future generations are included in the appeal which the passage we shall read to-morrow sets forth:—"Neither with you only do I make this covenant and this oath, but with him that standeth here with us this day before the Lord our God, and also with him that is not here with us this day" (xxix., 14). Hence his words have lost none of their significance, nothing of their freshness, during the three thousand years that have elapsed since their first utterance by Moses himself to the listening multitudes on the farther shores of Jordan. Even to-day their warning rolls to us across the centuries. We, too, are standing before the Lord our God.

The Last Sabbath in the Year.

This is the last Sabbath in the Jewish year numbered 5673. Another year, with its advantages, its privileges, its opportunities, and its failures, its joys and its sorrows, its trials and its compensations, is fast drawing to its close. In a few days it will have been swallowed up in the immeasurable gulf of time. Such an occasion is sufficiently impressive to warrant the application of the words with which Moses prefaced his last discourse: "Ye stand this day, all of you, before the Lord your God." Though the year through which we have passed is practically dead, to us Divine Providence vouchsafes a larger lease of life, and in a very real sense we are standing in the presence of Almighty God. At such a season religion bids us look back upon the road we have been travelling. It urges us to ponder the uses to which we ha

THE INDIAN EXPRESS

Madras Friday, June 27, 1975

Economic Notes

Blocked option

By BALRAJ MEHTA

Qaddafy behind Lebanon clashes, says Sadat

Aid-India consortium hears Kaul

Letters

A common failing

Censorship was always there where newspapers were: Censorship of Jewish Chronicle by Tsarist government (hereditary monarchy), September 26, 1913. Photo credit: The Story of Journalism by Elizabeth Grey, Longmans Young Books, London & Harlow, 1968 edition, page 15. (below) The Indian express of June 27, 1975, left its editorial blank in protest against censorship. Photo credit: Indianexpress.Com, Blank Editorial.

The Government was armed with a wide range of powers, which kept the press completely at its mercy (It was kept *in terrorium* during British Rule for many years (see Chapter two, sub- section "Hicky's Meteoric Rise and Mercurial Fall" for tools and techniques used to gag the press then). Apart from censorship which could be used for the near destruction of a newspaper or journal, it imposed a heavy security deposit (which no small journal could afford), provision was made for complete seizure of the printing presses after erring, and provision to jail individual journalists. Under the Board of Directors, "Guidelines" could be issued and threats conveyed orally on the telephone or through third parties. And then there were steps taken by Government to prevent the publication of any matter which it considered objectionable.[4] The Parliamentary Proceedings (Protection of Publication) Act, 1956, which came to be known as the Feroze Gandhi Act, was replaced by the notorious Prevention of Publication of Objectionable Matter Act. Thus, parliamentary proceedings became "objectionable". The Act, which came into force on February 11, 1976, applied not only to newspapers and periodicals but also to books, pamphlets and leaflets, either printed or duplicated. What constituted "objectionable" matter was sufficiently vague to give the interpreting authorities a wide range of arbitrary powers. The illiberal intentions of the Government became amply evident when the Act was placed beyond judicial scrutiny by its inclusion in the Ninth Schedule of the Constitution. Having placed the press totally at its mercy, the Government set about in compiling a code of conduct for journalists. The 14-point code of journalistic ethics was finalized at the All-India Newspaper Editor's Conference on April 30 and May 1, 1976, and laid on the Table of the Lok Sabha. Like the codes of conduct drafted by Vice-Chancellors for university teachers, the code for journalists contained everything, except the essential ingredient of the profession. Analyzing the code, V.K. Narasimhan pertinently asked,

"Is it by accident that nowhere…in the code of ethics, does the word 'freedom' appear?" Indeed, codes of conduct were thought of for everybody except the ruling politician who set themselves above all ethics![5]

From 1974, the Government was gunning for the removal of B. G. Verghese (a one-time Press Secretary to Mrs. Gandhi) from the editorship of the *Hindustan Times* A series of articles by the editor embarrassed and irritated the Government, with the result that political pressure at the highest level was brought to bear on K. K. Birla to remove Verghese from the editorship of the newspaper. The matter was taken up by the Press Council despite Birla's contention that the Council had no jurisdiction in such matters.[6]

In December 1975, the Press Council was abolished by a Presidential ordinance. The official explanation was that it had "generally dealt with complaints of a comparatively minor character" and could therefore be dispensed with! Another example of the Government's unethical behavior was the arrest in July of the journalist Kuldip Nayar under MISA (Maintenance of Internal Security Act) without giving any reason. But the bona fides of the order was questioned in the Delhi High Court, and in September, a two-member bench struck it down as illegal and unjustified since no specific charges had been levelled against him. Nayar was freed even before the judgment in the hope that the adverse verdict, which the Government expected, would not be pronounced. But Justice Rangarajan ignored what had happened and insisted on delivering his judgment. He pointed out that while under the Act, the reasons for the detention were not required to be disclosed, the Court could not give its verdict unless it had this information. The Government's reaction once again underlined the autocratic character of the regime. It lost no time in issuing an ordinance whereby there was no need to furnish information even to the Court. Justice Rangarajan himself was transferred to Gauhati.[7]

Mr. Vidya Charan Shukla, then Information and Broadcasting Minister, went about his job with hammer-handedness and the lack of scruple that defy description. He systematically set out to promote divisions in the ranks of the press to gather around him a coterie of journalistic sycophants who approved of everything he said or did, and to sponsor a series of measures intended to convert the entire Indian press in to a submissive appendage of the ruling party and the mouthpiece of Mrs. Gandhi. The power of censorship was abused in all possible ways. The distribution of advertisements was brazenly used as a weapon to penalize non-conforming papers.[8] Veteran journalists, who in the past had penned thundering articles, now cooed like sucking doves. They settle down to comforts of their cushy jobs with the thought that they could not after all do much. Some of them cringe and crawled.[9] The Government in its effort to do news management on February 1, 1976, merged four news-agencies in the country into a single group. These were the *Press Trust of India*, the *United News of India*, the *Hindustan Samachar* and the *Samachar Bharti*. It was part of the Orwellian double-talk of the emergency that this merger was described in the official Reference Manual as "voluntary".[10]

By the time Mrs. Gandhi was entrenched in power, the country had strayed far from the days of Mahatma Gandhi, who throughout his life had insisted on purity of means of politics. Her economic policies relating to controls and issuing of licenses were successfully used for raising election funds by dubious and corrupt ways.[11] The Goenkas had their interests in tea, chemicals, automobiles, cement and sugar and they owned the *Express* chain of papers. Likewise, Birlas, who owned the *Hindustan Times*, controlled tea, jute, textiles, automobiles, aluminum and consumer goods. Bennett Coleman and company of *The Times of India* had their interests in steel, heavy engineering, textile, coal, mining, paper, chemicals and consumer goods.[12] With government licensing policies and its efforts to check the concentration of economic power, the Indian press became vulnerable to attack on its freedom. What saved it from utter destruction, however, was the judiciary which struck down several governmental measures. [13]

It was during emergency that India's "Sovereign Democratic Republic" wore a new albeit clumsy look and country was declared to be "Sovereign, Socialist, Secular, Democratic Republic".

The original preamble enshrined "fraternity", assuring the dignity of individual and unity of nation. To "unity" was added "integrity" and it became "Unity and Integrity".

Three news words – "Socialist, Secular and Integrity" – were added to the preamble through the 42nd Amendment.

Nani Palkhivala commented:

> *"The architect of 42nd Amendment were anxious to make their philosophy as explicit as possible." Addition of these three words, Palkhivala said, "Anyone who has a sense of rhythm and style would know that beauty of preamble distinguished by economy of words would be marred by insertion of these words...you may well try to improve upon Shakespeare 'the rest is silence' into 'rest is complete, weird, and baffling silence'."*

Apart from newspapers, other news periodicals and some journals deserve to be mentioned here as fight of these periodicals attracted landmark judgements about freedom of the press in a democratic society and the citizen's right to know. Foremost of them was *Freedom First* edited by Minoo Masani. When Masani refused to accept the censor's verdict, he filed a writ petition in Bombay High Court, which was admitted on July 18, 1975. In November, Justice R P Bhatt struck down the censor's order finding nothing objectionable in the articles. The Government went in appeal and the case was heard before a division bench consisting of Justice D P Madon and Justice M H Kania, and the final judgement was delivered on February 10, 1976. The court upheld the censor's verdict with regard to two items out of eleven and dismissed the appeal. In their landmark judgement, the learned judges had observed:

"Logic rebels and reason revolts at interference so devoid of any foundation in reality or basis in common sense." In the course of the judgement, the Court expanded on the role of the press and the function of censorship. It said, "True democracy can only thrive in a free clearing house of competing ideologies and philosophies – political, economic and social and in this the press had an important role to play. The day this clearing house closes down would toll the death knell in the democracy. It is not the function of censor acting under the censorship order to make all newspapers and periodicals trim their sails to one wind or tow along the single file or to speak in chorus with one voice".[14]

Another historic judgement concerned *Bhumiputra*, a Gujarati periodical edited by Chunilal Vaidya from Baroda. It published M.C. Chagla's inaugural address to Civil Liberties, which invited show cause notice by the Chief Censor Harry J D Penha for confiscation of the issue and the forfeiture of the Yagna Mudrika press where it was printed. The judgment was delivered by Justice J.B. Mehta and Justice S.H. Sethi. The honorable bench observed:

"We feel unhappy to state that guidelines issued by the Chief Censor completely choke the pipeline of democracy, fully contaminate the otherwise clean and invigorating environment of freedom and have a strong tendency to create a Managerial Class for wire fencing of the people of this country to it. There cannot be more draconian assault on people in democracy than are which is disclosed in the guidelines issued by the Chief Censor."

The Court's order specifically stated that its verdict could not be censored, and any order to that effect would be illegal. The judges observed, "The Censor is not above the Court. It is necessary for it to realize that it is subject to the jurisdiction of the Court. What is held *ultra vires* cannot be allowed to operate as *intra vires* under the veil of secrecy. We cannot permit liberty of the people to be under the weight of censorship. We are not inclined to do anything by which deprivation of liberty can be continued even for a moment more."

The Court had done its work and contributed to the cause of liberty, but the servile press failed the country in its hour of need. In Ahmedabad, with the exception of *Sandesh* and *Jansatta*, none of the dailies carried the news of the judgment. The *Janmabhoomi* group of papers at Bombay, Surat, Rajkot and Bhuj furnished a summary; so did the *Mumbai Samachar* of Bombay and the *Gujaratmitra* of Surat.[15] The English dailies sinned by their silence. *The Times of India* was perhaps awestruck by editorial palsy or sclerosis of the journalistic conscience, for it generally refused to carry such items. Rightly was it derided as *The Times of Indira!*[16]

Maharashtra Times and *Economic Times* were other two dailies from the same house which lived up to their reputation. Akshay Kumar Jain, Chief editor of *NavbharatTimes*, Delhi, and Khushvant Singh, editor of *Illustrated Weekly of India*, Mumbai, of course, emerged as champions of the emergency within the house. Jain was quoted as pleading the Prime Minister, "to put press censorship on a more or less permanent footing as in his views the people of India were not yet mature to be entrusted with freedom." Singh once accompanied Ms. Maneka Gandhi to the Bombay's Times office when the case of Kissa Kursi Ka was heard in Mumbai. He also established Sanjay Gandhi as an icon of youth on basis of a poll conducted by the *Weekly*.

Press Commissions:

The commission was set up in September 1952 under the Chairmanship of Hon'ble C S Randhava. The commission submitted its first report in 1954. It made several important recommendations, like constitution of Press Council to look into the matters of the press on regular basis, appointment of wage board for working journalists and Registrar of Newspapers of India (RNI). The council, a statutory body with quasi-judicial power, was established on July 4, 1966. The office of RNI was created on July 1, 1956. The first Press Commission of India expressed mixed feelings about the "standards and performance" of the press.

It observed that despite shortcomings, such as yellow journalism, sensationalism, malicious attacks on public, indecency and vulgarity, the country possesses a number of newspapers of which any country may be proud of. Many journalists who appeared before the commission assured it that "if the responsibility of regulating the profession were left to the journalists themselves, they would maintain integrity of the profession and ensure that Indian journalism progresses along healthy lines." In its first full annual report (1967), the Press Council of India described the importance of its function thus: "The Council is intended not only to protect the freedom of the press but also the rights of citizens ensuring that they are served by a healthy, non-scurrilous, public-spirited and independent press. Adjudication of complaints against the behaviour of the press and also behaviour of others towards press thus constitutes the most important function the press council. The council is also impowered to hold hearing on receipt of a complaint and take suitable action where appropriate. It may either warn or censure the errant on finding guilty."

For the first time, a thorough inquiry into the structure and functioning of the press was made by the Press Commission during 1952–54. The Commission noted that there was a considerable degree of concentration of newspaper ownership and saw the danger of this tendency developing further. Among the many recommendations of the Commission to help the development of a healthy press, one was for the appointment of a Press Registrar.

The Second Press Commission was set up in May 1978 having Justice P C Goswami as Chairman. But the commission resigned in January 1980 and was reconstituted in April 1980 and submitted its report in 1982. The continuation of the Press Council of India was agreed upon. In its report, the commission strongly recommended the delinking of the press from its connections with other industries. The Commission clarified that it viewed journalism not merely as an industry but as a public service and profession.

One of the major recommendations of the Commission was for setting up of a National Development Commission (NDC) to promote the growth of the entire Indian press. NDC was to set up as advisory assistance, especially to small and medium newspapers for the development of printing and other technologies suitable for them. Yet another important recommendation was with regard to news to advertisement ratio. It suggested 60:40 rates for big papers, 50:50 for medium and 40:60 for small papers.

It has been observed that ownership and control of the press does not rest within the industry; the present managements have vested interests and strong connections outside the industry. The linkages are strong. The desirability of delinking of ownership of the Indian press from big business and monopoly capital has been emphasized repeatedly. It has also been suggested that newspaper industry should be able to play a positive role in socio-economic processes to further national development. How do we achieve these and what are the alternatives? To delink the press from big business, one obvious alternative could be public takeover of the top eight newspaper establishments.

The Press Commission made some startling revelations about the state of the media in the country. It stated that most of the so- called small papers are a threat to real journalism. "The producers of these papers do not even need money to become a public menace. They need no press and no permanent staff. Not confined to small papers, the malady has made inroads into medium papers and papers run even by big establishments. The phenomenon was not completely unknown before. But there used to be some semblance of propriety even in the absentee landlordism of the editor who used to compete with public men in getting his photographs published in the paper. Today, norms are violated with impunity. Designating themselves as editors or adjectivised as 'managing' editor, the neo-literates determine the newspaper's policy and its projection. They appoint their agents on key positions to disfigure events and dictate terms. Freedom of press to them means freedom to distribute muck when the people sip their morning tea. They are the adulterators of the worst order. A peculiar mixture in being manufactured with the blending of managerial and editorial functions promoting unholy alliance with other anti-social elements including discredited politician and corrupt officials. The editor's canvass advertisement support and work out case for enhanced rates. Failure to oblige them is fraught with adverse reports in their papers. If this massive raid by trespassers is allowed to go unchallenged, the professional journalists will be wiped out from top positions and replaced by *polythene editors*."

The Committee points out that not only journalism but social life as well is being polluted by this development, "newspaper is more than an industry. Whether officially declared or not, it is a public trust. Besides building public opinion, a newspaper has therefore to be also responsive to it. It cannot be one-way traffic."

All commercial aspects of newspapers and magazines, such as advertising, circulation, and sales management, are efficiently and effectively organized. With an increase in literacy rates, rise in incomes, greater thirst for news, newspapers in all languages look forward to a bright future.

Science and technology not only helped in the proliferation of newspapers but also provided the necessary tools for sturdy growth and evolution of the newspaper business. Multiplying circulations and swelling advertising revenues now beckon newspaper proprietors. Given such an important role and place in the society, it is in public interest to ensure that press in a country should be free from control of any one interest group; press should not be owned, controlled or dominated by any one vested interest, particularly a private one. It is obvious that ownership and control structure of a newspaper establishment would determine the character of the news reports, style and news display, and the editorial view-point and other comments. What gets reported is of significance, but it is of equal importance as to what gets "blacked out". News reports are not only known to be a view from the clouded window but these are very often presented according to the preferred "colour" of the newspaper managements.

The need for a study of the Indian press establishments to determine their ownership character and other business associations is only too obvious. Press, besides being an industry by itself, has wide socio-economic and political potential. It is well known that political newspapers and journals invariably run in losses and yet their publications are not discontinued. In more than one way, direct benefits reaped by newspaper owners are of much lesser relevance than the power that goes with ownership and control of a widely circulated newspaper. Many of the newspapers would indeed be under loss, and therefore, face threat of closure if the owners did not transfer assured advertisements and other patronage from their own or other associate industrial and commercial enterprises. Newspaper industry is heavily dependent on revenue from advertisements since prices of newspapers have to be kept low for various reasons. For obtaining advertisements, the newspaper establishments have to woo their advertisers. It is because the absence of any set norms for allocation expenditure and its distribution is more a matter of discretion and patronage than an act aiming at genuine publicity for spread of information to consumers. The degree of truth in the above statement is borne out by the fact that many political parties found bringing out of 'souvenirs' rewarding to raise funds from corporations. When a newspaper establishment is owned and controlled by an industrial conglomerate, it can easily be made into an economically viable one through assured advertisements and other job work. It is because of this reason that newspaper industry and its economics can only be understood in the overall framework of ownership and control structure and other linkages of individual establishment. We believe that control over press is not sought only for the limited objective of earning high rates of financial returns on investments. The objectives are much wider, particularly for national monopoly houses.

Historically, many newspapers in India were established during the national struggle for independence. A large number of the editors and founders were politically motivated and brought out their newspapers to educate and mobilize public opinion for the struggle. They were not motivated by business or profits considerations. This also explains the phenomenon of trust in the newspaper industry. However, during the past three decades, in most cases the politically inspired newspaper establishments have lost their old character. Many of the erstwhile small newspaper establishments have disappeared. The ones which survived have diversified their activities to other industries or the ownership have changed hands. As a consequence of these developments, the relative significance of private industry associated with newspapers has increased in a noticeable manner.

The changing character in ownership and control structures of the Indian press has far reaching socio-economic implications. It is of common knowledge that press-reporters and senior staff of many newspapers are also employed to promote non-newspaper interests of their managements. Inspired news stories are timed and planted to influence decision making in Government. While use of press for promotion of house interest is known, it is not very often realized that newspaper managements exercise their choice to ignore or build up public images of chosen political personalities.

During the last two decades, dailies in all languages have set up editions in such remote places where people could not even dream of seeing copies of newspapers earlier. Besides, some newspapers have started sister publications in several local languages. For example, the *Indian Express* group, besides its English daily edition, used to publish from 16 centers in the country, owned a paper each in Tamil, Gujarati, Hindi, Telugu, Kannada, and Marathi. It also owned a financial daily and a film weekly (in three languages). Similarly, the *Ananda Bazar Patrika* group has a paper each in Bengali and English, a financial daily, a fortnightly each on cinema, sports, economics and commerce. Hindi newspapers *Aaj, Jagran, Bhaskar, Nav Bharat, Rajasthan Patrika* and many others come out from more than half a dozen towns. *Rajasthan Patrika* has one edition from Bangalore. One can safely predict a bright future for the Indian press in the 21st century.

Martin Luther's 95 Theses: The First Voice of Dissent

5

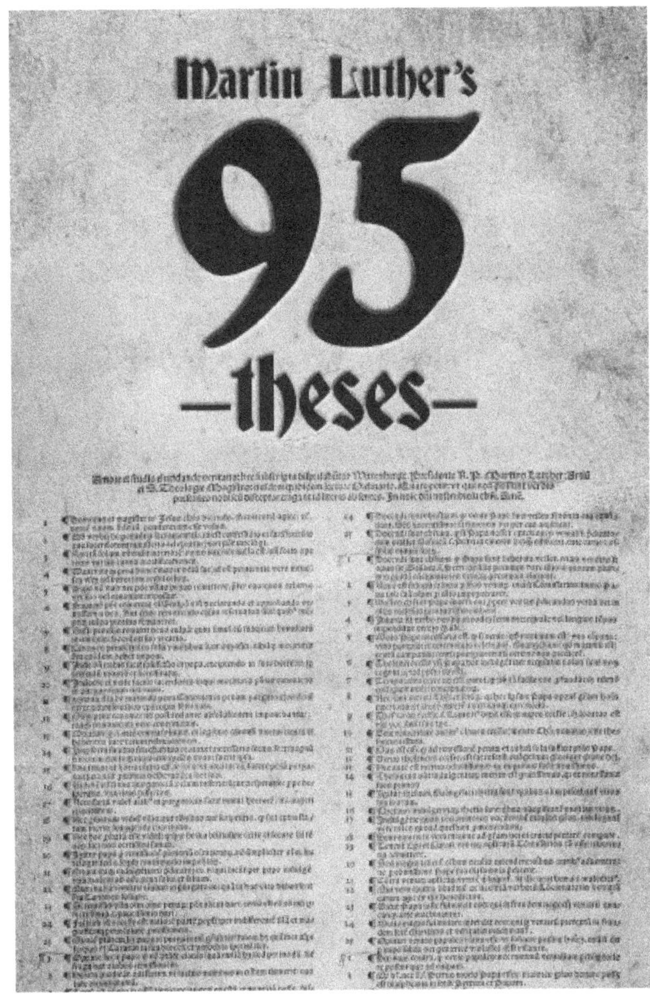

Martin_Luther_and_95 these-1-the First voice of dissent. Courtesy Olive Tree Bible Software.

Humans are gifted by nature with ultimate communication abilities. Humans started speaking, and then jotting down things on stone or whatever material they could possibly found. This paved the way for stability in life, which later on helped in the growth of civilization around the world. In traditional societies most of the knowledge came through oral tradition. Many forms of such knowledge have still been kept alive. Written form came thereafter.

Once humans settled, endeavors were made to write down the knowledge. We can understand the need to express, which resulted in the invention of paper, ink and even movable type. All these inventions were made in China, and the first newspaper on silk was also made possible in China. The movable type developed by the Chinese was made of clay that disintegrated with time. Moreover, the inventor Bi-Sheng had to work in a language that had 5000 characters. He developed it 400 years before German goldsmith Gutenberg developed the movable metal type. Gutenberg drew heavily from such previous experiences and developed something that opened the gate of public domination over knowledge. Gutenberg's remarkable machine gave information an escape velocity, and knowledge was put into the public domain. Martin Luther was the first to register a voice of dissent based on Gutenberg's remarkable machine. He got his historic *Ninety-five These*s composed in movable metal type and many copies were printed on the printing machine. This was a turning point in human history. For the first time a single person challenged the powerful Roman Catholic Church and became successful. Though he was excommunicated, but in his life time he saw almost whole of North Europe turning Protestant. Martin Luther was just 38 then. This indicated the huge power embedded in information waiting to explode at the right time and at the right place. But newspaper did not happen soon enough. It had to wait for more than 100 years before ancestors of the modern newspaper were born. Newspapers changed the narrative of public discourse forever. It broke the inertia of cold indifference and made the common man an active Martin Luther's 95 Theses: The First Voice of Dissent participant in the system of governance in countries around the world. So, the beginning was not a smooth ride for newspapers in any country. Every Government saw it with suspicion since no one in power likes to be criticized or made accountable for. The powerful Roman Catholic Church could not have imagined that someone could put questions uncomfortable to them. But wrongdoings or monopolistic attitude of a society has to be corrected in the larger interest of the society. This is what newspapers precisely stand for. People in power did everything to manipulate and some Governments are still doing it, but this is like not learning from history.

So, no wonder that in India, initial attempts to bring out a newspaper was thwarted. Another effort took thirteen long years to bear fruit. But, as if two years of *Hicky's Gazette* was more than enough, the British East India Company could tolerate it no more. The Company looked for a paper that could toe its line. And there were more than enough newspapers that were prepared to do that. However, the seed of dissent was sown. Against this backdrop Indian press had to undertake an arduous journey, negotiate with the worst kind of administrative manageability, face an unscalable tyranny, but it survived. Indian press can be proud of its legacy. It attracted the finest of minds bubbling with patriotism of the highest order. Most of the editors who worked for *Ghadar* were freedom fighters, and many of them faced the ultimate punishment from an autocratic foreign rule.

Ghaderites planned an armed rebellion when the British were engaged in the First World War. The political situation in Indian had changed. In temples and gurudwaras prayers were being held for British victory. But the architects of Ghadar movement were not war-strategists. They could not prevent leakage of information, which resulted in the ultimate catastrophe. Our heart goes out to them. It has been truly said, "Indian war of Independence was not fought with gun but with newspapers and journals" – credit for this ought to be given to men whose integrity was of the highest order.

With the gradual shift from oral communication to written and from written to printed, quantum of information kept increasing exponentially.

Gutenberg's machine was so perfect that it basically remained unchanged for almost 500 years. It only changed when another medium with much more openness and increased quantum capacity arrived – the internet. The best part of these media is that one succeeding medium does not completely erase the preceding ones. They coexisted and were effortlessly used in combination for the larger good. It is certain that media will go as far as science and technology will take it to. Human desire to communicate has immense potential that needs to be explored much further, and with continued development in science and technology, more vehicles of information will be invented which will take humanity to still uncharted territories. Who knows?

Epilogue

6

What does a newspaper do for a society? Way back in 1878, at the launch of *Bharat Mitra* on May 17, its editor Laxmi Narain Garde had addressed readers in the following words:

> *"What positive changes a newspaper brings about, is clear once we see Bombay and Bengal, (in other places) .... where newspaper is not in vogue, hope of progress is like hoping against hope. It's a tool that easily brings entire world before you even in closed doors. If there was no newspaper how would an administrator come to know the condition of the people, and wouldn't it lead to a chaos in his administration! Thus, a civilized and people-friendly ruler always encourages success of a newspaper in his regime."*

As it has been pointed out in the book, the voice of dissent that started its journey with Martin Luther's *Ninety-five Theses* has really come a long way since then. Governments around the world had a tough time in coming to terms with this product of science and technology, which was the ultimate empowerment tool for the masses. In India, too, the first effort to bring out a newspaper was thwarted. Hicky could run his famous paper *Hicky's Gazette* for merely two years. Government did not like his "open to all" stance. Hicky was termed by some contemporary as "blessed by nature with considerable talent, but quite uneducated and violent in temper, especially when apposed or thwarted in any of his wild plans." We will never know how true it was; but the way he was silenced questions the real intent of the administration. His heavy dues were reduced to a miniscule amount. Hicky possessed a doggedness and persistence in face of all calamities, which speaks well of the trader- printer-turned journalist. He proved to be a John Wilkes (the journalist who fought for the freedom of the press in Britain) for India. The Government did not stop here itself. It wanted newspapers to toe its line. Soon, printers and publishers were competing against each other in vowing to serve the Government very obediently and humbly. A point came when the Government thought of bringing out its own newspaper. In 1801, Wellesley, the then governor, had come to the conclusion that the establishment of an official gazette would be the best method of "silencing" the existing printing media, which was an evil of the first magnitude, useless to literature and to the public, dubiously profitable to the speculators. This scheme was ultimately abandoned on the grounds of cost involved.

Governments have often tried to have its own newspapers. After independence, Government of Maharashtra furnished a proposal to the Centre in which it said, "It has been noticed that some of the newspapers, particularly belonging to big groups, deliberately indulge in a sensational manner of reporting…the prejudicial criticism levelled by opposition receives undue importance and disproportionate space in all these newspapers. These newspapers even go to the extent of creating imaginary stories capable of demoralising the whole administration and creating a situation leading to insecurity." However, this plan of the Maharashtra Government also could not see fruition.

Press matured much early in Europe, but not without some criticism of very high order.

Honoré de Balzac, 1840

"In France, the press is the fourth power of state, it attacks all, yet no one attacks it. It reprimands recklessly. It asserts a domination over politician and men of letters that is not reciprocated, claiming that it is protagonist and sacred. They say and do horribly wrong things, and that are their right! It is high time we took a look at these unknown, second rate men who hold such importance in their time and who are moving force behind a press."

"The press has become the most powerful force in western countries. It has surpassed in power the executive, legislative and judiciary."

Alexander Solzhenitsyn, Harvard University, June 1978.

(Quoted in *Attitudes About Media, A five century comparison* by Lawrence Parisot in Media Power and Politics by Doris A Gaber, Second edition, Macmillan India, 1990, Reprinted with permission of American Enterprise Institute for Public Policy Research)

Huge faith and public trust reposed in media was bound to invite criticism from its ardent critics in intelligentsia as well as public. So, it was in constant public gaze. Also, social scientists from around the world have studied the impact of the media on society. Max Weber, Noam Chomsky and Walter Lipman are among many who have studied it in detail.

Walter Lipmann in his classic study on newspaper says, "Journalist point a flashlight rather than a mirror at the world." Accordingly, the audience does not receive the complete image of a scene; it gets a highly selective series of glimpses instead. Reality is tainted. Lipmann also explained why media cannot possibly tell the truth objectively as truth is subjective and entails more probing and explanation which the hectic pace of news production hardly allows.

Therefore, on the whole, the quality of news about modern society is an index of its social organization. The better the institution, more or all interest concerned are formally represented, more issues are disentangled, more objective criteria are introduced, more perfectly an affair can be presented as news. At its best, the press is a servant and guardian of the institution; at its worst, it is a means by which a few people exploit social disorganizations to their own ends. In the degree to which institutions fail to function, the unscrupulous journalist can fish in troubled waters.

Mahatma Gandhi was against using press for profit. He brought with him high ethical and moral values to the Indian press. During the time of freedom struggle, social responsibilities associated with publishing outweighed all commercial considerations. Mahatma did not live long to suggest ways and means by which sustainability of the press could be ensured. Clearly, putting aside all commercial consideration was not the answer. As Lipmann has further noted in his study of newspapers, "It has become a beam of searchlight that recklessly moves about, bringing one episode after another out of darkness in to the vision. Society cannot be governed by episodes, eruption and incidents. It is only when press works by a steady light of its own that is when it is turned upon them, reveals a situation intelligible enough for a popular decision. The trouble lies deeper than the press and so does the remedy."

In India, there have been two Press Commissions since independence to look in to the affairs of the Indian press. Press Commissions had found enough anomalies that have crept in following the independence. Some revelations are startling and seem to be a direct outcome of leaving commercial considerations of media to settle on its own. Basic frames like who could be a journalist or editor, or who could own, operate and publish a newspaper became so fluid that just anybody could get in.

The Indian press could not take the shape of a firm institution where rules, regulation and discipline were to be followed.

"The Report Committee appointed by UP Government in January, 1975 to go in to the reorganisation of the State Information Department contained several instances of the malpractices indulged in by some newspapers."

The report says that the help given to small newspapers has had unforeseen results. Like "bad money drives good money out of circulation", many of these small newspapers are making it increasingly difficult for genuine newspapers and newsmen to survive. They have better access to the seat of power. Their visits to Information Department are more frequent. They knew the art of *Sam-Dam-Dand–Bhed*. Their actual periodicity is generally determined by their need to harass or oblige some individuals.

"Of the 57 dailies (approved for Government advertisements), 34 did not subscribe to any news agency. Of the 72 dailies from the state more than half seem to be casual production. They do not subscribe to any recognised news agency and generally do not have permanent staff. They hire temporary/ part-time hands that need not be paid according to statutory requirements. Some big newspapers have also been circumventing Wage Board provision." The report says, "No newspaper should be eligible to receive Government advertisement, if it does not conform to regulations protecting the rights of its employees and if, it fabricates details in respect of circulation, staff etc." The report further says that "We saw three dailies in Meerut, having different titles and identical matter. We saw in Moradabad a new experiment of the same sheet producing two papers. On one side was a Hindi title with one registration number, on the other side an Urdu publication with a different registration number. None of these could be called a newspaper but their resourceful editors had secured registration number from the office of Registrar of newspapers for India. In at least one case, the editor had given his thumb impression on the Declaration form."

This cannot be true about each and every press institution in the country, but the Commission's observation that "bad money drives good money out of circulation" should get due attention.

Big business houses that have no issue with quality of staff or working conditions, but a corporate entity owning a media house having other business interests was a crucial issue with the Press Commission. The Commission could not find any of the eight big media houses having a single business interest that is media. It went to suggest public takeover of these eight business media houses.

This was clear around the eighties that all was not well with the fourth estate in India. And if the problem was not addressed, the situation was going to deteriorate much further. This was when electronic media started taking shape in the country.

True, the task is not easy. It is difficult, but that is what a mass media or newspaper establishment is all about. Neither should the press be converted from an instrument of "dissent" in to a "consent manufacturing factory" nor should its commercial interest outweigh all social responsibilities attached to it.

Appendix I : Monitoring of Indian Newspapers & Journals in London

Indian newspaper Reports; C. 1868-1942 From British Library London.

Part I : Bengal; 1874–1903

Part 2: Bengal; 1904-1916

Part 3: Punjab; Agra, Oudh, Rajputana & Central Province: 1868-1942

Part 4: United Provinces: 1897-1937

Part 5: Madras:1876-1921

Part 6: Bombay; 1874-1898

From 1858 until independence in 1947, the British Government ruled India with two administrative systems: the British Provinces, comprising around 60 per cent of the country and totally under British control, and the Indian (princely) states which recognized British rule in return for local autonomy, comprising around 40 per cent of the country. The material in Part 4 of this microfilm project covers reports for the United Provinces, 1897–1937. In 1833 the Bengal Presidency had been divided into two parts. The north-western part became the Presidency of Agra, which in 1836 was renamed the North-Western Provinces and placed under a Lieutenant-Governor. The kingdom of Oudh was annexed in 1856 and placed under a Chief Commissioner. In 1877 the North-Western Provinces and Oudh were joined together under a single administration. Their name was changed to the United

Provinces of Agra and Oudh in 1902 and shortened to the United Provinces in 1912 with the city of Lucknow at their center. In 1947 the United Provinces became a province of the new independent India, and its name was changed to Uttar Pradesh. It should be noted that the reports for the period up until 1902 are described as being from the native newspapers published in the North-Western Provinces and Oudh. Lord Ripon's repeal of Lytton's Vernacular Press Act in 1881 coincided with the abolition of the Press Commissionership. The relaxation in the attempted exercise of political control by the British over the press in India opened the way for vigorous debate on the future of India. The writings of the Indian intelligentsia found their way into an increasing number of new newspapers, both Anglo-Indian and vernacular. The increasingly active independence movement later formed into two separate camps in 1907. There was the "Garam Dal" (the extremists or "hot" faction) of Bal Gangadhar Tilak, who founded the Marathi daily *Kesari* (The Lion), and the "Naram Dal" of Gopal Krishna Gokhale (the moderates or "soft" faction). The development of the independence movement can be followed in the newspapers of the early part of the twentieth century. The Indian National Congress, also known as the Congress Party, was formed in 1885. It comprised chiefly of members of the Western-educated professional elite. Public opinion had started to turn against the British Government of India and it sought to represent the views of the populace from both urban and rural areas. There was an undercurrent of feeling that British rule was unfair, and this is reflected in the newspaper reports contained in this collection. Agitation and disturbances in the streets were common and the media played a huge role in re-enforcing feelings of real and imagined grievances. After the First World War, the Congress Party was taken over by socialists like Jawaharlal Nehru and Subhash Chandra Bose who had more extreme views. Later it became associated with Mahatma Gandhi, who, although never a member of the party, became its spiritual leader. Under Gandhi's influence, the party became the true representative of the people by working against caste differences, untouchability, poverty, and religious and ethnic boundaries. In the 1930s there was a series of conferences in London where the making of a new constitution in India was discussed, finally taking the form of the 1935 Government of India Act. All these subjects are discussed in the reports. The press in cities such as Agra, Lucknow, Kanpur, Oudh, Allahabad and Varanasi played a significant role in the growth of nationalism after the Indian National Congress was formed in 1885. Improvements in education fostered the exchange of ideas and aspirations for liberty from foreign rule. The Congress Party was an umbrella organization, consisting of socialists, traditionalists, and even Hindu and Muslim conservatives, but it was fundamentally a Hindu-dominated organization. The majority of the Muslims did not trust the Hindu majority, and in 1900 when the British Government made Hindi the official language of the United Provinces, there was consternation among the Muslims that the Hindu majority would suppress Muslim culture and religion. In 1906 thirty- five leading members of the Muslim community gathered in Shimla and presented their demands to the then Viceroy Lord Minto. The All- India Muslim League comprising 56 members was created as a result of this meeting. Although initially the League's intention was to remain loyal to the British Government, it changed its views to a desire for independence in 1913 when the British decided to create a united state of Bengal. The headquarters of the League was in Lucknow and Aga Khan was elected as its first president. Its goal at this stage was not to establish an independent state but to promote understanding between the Muslim community and other Indians. In 1930, however, the leader of the League Sir Muhummad Iqbal first put forward the demand for a separate Muslim state in India to be known as Pakistan, and after many years of discussions and conferences, the state of Pakistan became a reality in 1947. The 1930s were an important period in India's history. The population had been growing since the early 1920s and there was pressure on India's natural resources. The number of towns grew considerably but the majority of the Indian populace were still villagers. The new Indian entrepreneurs were men from communities with business experience. All these factors affected political decisions and led to the growth in nationalist feelings. All of the topics are well covered in the newspaper reports.

Indian Newspaper Reports

The Indian newspaper reports from the Asia, Pacific and Africa Department at the British Library constitute an important series to be found in the Record Department, Papers of the Oriental and India Office Collections. The reports consist of abstracts taken from Anglo- Indian and vernacular newspapers from different regions of India.

The reports were compiled weekly and consisted of typewritten abstracts of the contents of Indian newspapers with some extracts translated by an official translator whose name is given at the end of the week's report. Each weekly report gives a list of both the Indian and the English language newspapers examined, with their place of publication, periodicity, number of subscribers, the names of the publisher, the circulation and the date of the issues examined. An extremely wide variety of newspapers were looked at weekly and later reports covering around 200 newspapers and periodicals were prepared. The reports list the languages of the newspapers, for example, Bengali, English and Bengali, English and Urdu, Bengali and Hindi, Hindi and Persian. Later reports give additional information such as the annual subscription charge, the names of the publisher and the printer and general remarks on the newspaper. For instance, "*The Zul Qarain* deals with educational and social matters of the Muslim community and political matters also…"

Part 4: United Provinces, 1897–1937

The newspaper reports included in **Part 4** cover years from 1897–1937. The abstracts and extracts contained in the reports will provide scholars with an invaluable insight into Indian social and political events, the conditions of the Indian and British population, criticisms of the British Government and the rapid development of nationalist feelings.

Examples of newspapers that were closely examined are:

- *Central Hindu College Magazine* Benares, circulation of 5,500 copies monthly
- *Advocate*, Lucknow, tri-weekly
- *Ranga Iyer*, Madras, circulation of 1,100 copies
- *Student World*, Lucknow, circulation of 450 copies monthly
- *Indian Daily Telegraph*, Lucknow, circulation of 500 daily
- *Leader*, Allahabad, circulation of 2,500 daily
- *Aligarh*, Aligarh, circulation of 840 monthly
- *Ifada*, Agra, circulation of 250 monthly
- *Zamara*, Cawnpore (Kanpur), circulation of 1,700 monthly
- *Indu*, Benares, circulation of 600 monthly
- *Trishul*, Benares circulation of 1,000 monthly

The abstracts contained in the reports are generally divided into the following sections:

I. Politics – foreign and home

II. Afghanistan &Trans-Frontier

III. Native States

IV. Administration

V. Legislation

VI. Railway

VII. Post Office

VIII. Native Societies & Religious & Social Matters

IX. Miscellaneous

The reports contain a wealth of information on topics as diverse as:

- The Defense of India Act
- The work of the Indian National Congress
- Land taxation
- The industrialization of India
- The United Provinces Municipalities Act
- The activities of the Muslim League and of the Liberal Federation
- News on the Indian States
- Political reforms
- The Labour Government
- Hindu–Muslim relations
- Unemployment and poverty
- Activities of the nationalist movement and its leaders
- Social legislation
- The death of Queen Victoria, 1901
- The Labour Commission
- Civil disobedience
- The Legislative Assembly
- The Partition of Bengal
- The sale of opium in Ceylon
- The workings of the Press Act and the imprisonment of newspaper editors
- The death of Edward VII and the coronation of George V
- Raids on the North-West Frontier
- The Non-Cooperation movement and the repressive policy of The Government
- The Trades Union Congress
- The Bengal Youth League
- The activities of Nehru and Gandhi
- Shia–Sunni riots

The literate population in India was still very small, even by 1900. But it was undeniable that from 1870 onwards, the number of Indian newspapers and journals proliferated. Most were in native languages and had small print runs and a local circulation. By 1885, Lawrence James suggested that there were some 319 different vernacular titles along with 96 English language newspapers. Most native newspapers were cheap weeklies. Personal abuse of officials was commonplace; one of the Punjabi newspapers attacked the province's Lieutenant Governor, Sir George Campbell, as "the baboon Campbell with a hairy body…His eyes flash forth in anger and his tail is all in flames". Many of the English language press, with a predominantly European readership, were equally quick to launch attacks on the pronouncement of the Indian National Congress. Kipling's old newspaper *The Allahabad Pioneer* (circulation 5,000) and the *Lahore Civil and Military Gazette* (circulation 4,000) were both virulent mouthpieces of British Government propaganda. During the First World War, positive publicity was crucial and the exploits of Indian soldiers were reported in glowing terms.

The following extracts taken from the reports show the development of nationalism:

The following are from the reports for 1901:

The Indian Appeal (Benares) of the 10th May says: Many of us will agree with the Viceroy when he told the Muhammedans, that the twentieth century was certain, whatever else it might bring forth, to be a century of great intellectual activity, of far reaching scientific discovery, and of probable unparalleled invention. That is all very grand. But what part are the Indians going to play in this intellectual arena….?"

The Roznamcha-i-Qaisari (Allahabad), of the 15th September, complains that "it would seem that a European gentleman has kicked a native to death near Allahabad Railway Station. It is a pity that the life of a native is considered to be of no more value than that of a pariah dog. In what a helpless condition the natives are! May God, have mercy on them!. "

The following is from the reports for 1910:

The editor of the *Karmayogi*" (Allahabad) writes: "There are many obstacles in the way of Indian nationalists.... Indians, should however, never loose courage for no nation was created to occupy forever a subordinate position in this universe. Even those that are ruled over by foreigners today have a right to govern and manage their own affairs themselves.... The editor reminds his readers that numerous hardships and sufferings will have to be borne and manifold virtues cultivated before India can rise higher in the state of nations...."

The following is from the reports for 1916:

The Prem (Brindaban, Muttra- *Read Mathura)* of the 26th July 1916 publishes a poem by Judh Singh Varma deploring the degraded condition of Indians as represented by their abject poverty, starvation, sectarian strifes, and mutual animosities, in the decay of their trade and industry, in the prevalence of famine and disease and in their social degeneration. They have already been reduced to helplessness by the imposition of taxes. He exhorts them to shake off indolence, to spread education in the country, to be united for mutual service, to give up evil social customs, to cultivate physical culture and to be self-respecting and self-confident. They should take to trade and industry. They should not hanker after jobs, but seek independence.

The extracts below are from the reports for January 1928 regarding the Muslim League and the Liberal Federation:

Very few papers had so far commented on the proceedings of the Muslim League. *The Leader* writes: "The split in the Muslim League will be regretted by those who attach greater importance to communal than national unity..." *The Indian Daily Telegraph* writes:- "In spite of the great shortcomings which were the outcome of the mischievous anti-national activities of the Shaffian clique the Calcutta session of the All-Indian Muslim League was a great success...."

The Leader writes: "The address delivered by Sir Tej Bahadur Sapru as President of the National Liberal Federation of India at Bombay is a master-piece. The whole of the address will be read by our countrymen not only with satisfaction but with pride. It ought to be read by Englishmen with a sense of deep humiliation. But people in whom there is no humility cannot easily be shamed into a confession of wrong-doing...."

The following is from the reports for 1936:

> *".....Muslim papers condemn the socialistic & revolutionary programme advocated by Mr. Nehru and regard it as being calculated to lead to anarchy and a bloody civil war... Some Muslim papers deplore the paucity of Muslims in the Congress and advise them to join it provided it abandons its anti-Muslim attitude and socialistic policy.... The Daily Pratap regards Pt. Nehru's address as a reflection of his career and says that every word of it bears the stamp of sincerity and honesty...."*

Appendix II: Circulation of Selected Dailies- Big, Medium and Small – At the Place of Publication-1979

BIG DAILIES Circulattion 75,000 and above. (Table 1)

S. No.	Name	Total Circulation	Circulation at the place of publication	Percentage
1	2	3	4	6
1.	Ananda Bazar. Patrika (Bengali), Calcutta	4,17,091	2,11,634	50.74
2.	Navbharat Times, (Hindi), Delhi	3,14,062	1,43,663	45.74
3.	Jagantar (Bengali), Calcutta	3,02,276	1,55,472	51.43
4.	Hindustan Times (English), Delhi	2,82,606	1,53,402	54.28
5.	Lok Satta (Marathi), Bombay	2,49,021	1,70,145	68.33
6.	Times of India (English), Bombay	2,40,039	1,83,546	76.47
7.	Malayala Manorama (Malayalam), Kottayam	2,23,023*	16,592	07.44
8.	Statesman (English) Calcutta	2,07,021*	1,02,652	49.59
9.	Hindustan (Hindi), Delhi	2,08,166	43,357	20.83
10.	Times of India (English), Delhi	1,74,102	57,667	33.12
11.	Total	26,17,407	12,38,130	47..30

Appendix II: Circulation of Selected Dailies- Big, Medium and Small – At the Place of Publication-1979

MEDIUM DAILIES Circulation >25,000 to <75,000 (Table 2)

1	2	3	4	6
1.	Pioneer (English), Lucknow	49,608	26,587	53.59
2.	Free press Journal (English), Bombay	49,040	36,521	74.47
3.	Indian Express (English), Madras	47,863*	26,363	55.08
4.	Hindu (English), Coimbatore	43,611*	9,783	20.55
5.	Times of India (English), Ahmedabad	46,978	19,292	41.07
6.	Sanmarg (Hindi), Culcutta	45,800	34,845	76.08
7.	Dinamalar (Tamil), Tirunelveli	45,703*	3,506	07.67
8.	Decan Chronicle (English) Secunderabad	42,437	37,004	87.20
9.	Mumbai Sakal (Marathi), Bombay	42,025*	23,009	54.74
10.	Statesman (English), New Delhi	41,338*	22,149	53.58
11.	Total	4,58,403	2,39,059	52.15

Source: A B C Certificates – January to December, 1979

(Total circulation of dailies with (*) taken from press in India, 1980 since ABC certificates did not indicate edition-wise circulation)

SMALL DAILIES, Circulation up to 25,000. (Table 3)

1	2	3	4	6
1.	Andhra Bhoomi (Telugu) Secunderabad	14,562	6,249	42.91
2.	Deaily Thanthi (Tamil), Salem	13,796*	3,600	26.53
3.	Economic Times (English), Calcutta	12,432	6,653	53.52
4.	Hindustan (Sindhi), Bombay	12,274	3,977	32.40
5.	Ranchi Express (Hindi), Ranchi	11,895	8,275	69.57
6.	Siasat Jadid (Urdu), Kanpur	11,571	5,015	43.34
7.	Naveen Dunia (Hindi), Jabalpur	8,092	3,983	49.22
8.	Total	84,622	37,812	44.68

Appendix II: Circulation of Selected Dailies- Big, Medium and Small – At the Place of Publication-1979

Total Number of newspapers for which circulation data was notavailable from 1963 to 1979 (Table 4) DEFAULTERS

Year	Total No. of newspapers	No. of newspapers for which		Per centage of defaulters
		Circulation data is available	Circulation dateis not available	
1	2	3	4	5
1963	7,790	5,888	1,902	24.4
1964	8,186	5,625	2,536	31.1
1965	7,906	5,972	1,934	24.5
1966	8,640	6,173	2,467	37.4
1967	9,315	6,308	3,007	32.4
1968	10,019	7,671	3,348	33.4
1969	10,281	6,353	3,928	38.2
1970	11,936	6,483	4,553	41.2
1971	12,218	6,634	5,584	45.7
1972	11,826	7,493	4,433	37.2
1973	12,653	8,055	4,598	36.3
1974	12,185	7,459	4,726	38.8
1975	12,423	7,914	4,509	37.1
1976	13,320	7,537	5,783	43.4
1977	14,531	7,763	6,768	46.6
1978	15,814	8,146	7,668	48.5
1979	17,168	8,052	9,116	53.1

Appendix III: List of Newspapers & Journals Published in India and Abroad 1780-1947

શ્રી

મુમબઈનાં શમાચાર

Almost two centuries old and still going strong, Mumbai Samachar First page of the first issue, 1822, Photo credit: wikipedia.org/wiki/bombay-samachar.

List of Indian newspapers & Journals, both English and Vernacular published in India and abroad since Hicky Gazette with press laws that directly affected freedom of speech and expression (1780-1947)

Year	Name of the paper	Founder/Founding Editor
1780	Hicky's Bengal Gazette *OR The Original Calcutta General Advertiser*-English/ Weekly/Calcutta	J A Hicky, 1st newspaper of the subcontinent.
1782	Indian Gazette- English/Weekly/ Calcutta	B Messink, Peter Reed
1785	*Madras Courier*- English/Weekly/ Madras	Hugh Boyden, R. William.
1784	Calcutta Gazette *OR Oriental Advertiser* – English/Weekly/ Calcutta	Francis Goldwin (Under Govt.Patronage).
1791	*Bombay Gazette*- English/Weekly/ Bombay	M D Cruz.
1795	*Bengal Hurkaru (...And Chronicle)* English/Weekly» Daily/Calcutta	Samuel Smith.
1785	*Madras Courier*- English/Weekly/Madras	Hugh Boyden, R. William.
1815	*Govt. Gazette*- English/Weekly/ Calcutta	Bengal Military Orphan Society.
1818	*Calcutta Journal* (*Chronicle*)- English /Bi-Weekly/ Calcutta	James Silk Buckingham* and thenMr. Sandy.
1818	*The Friends of India*- English/Monthly/ Calcutta.	Joshua Marshman.
1821	*Samvad Kaumudi*- English/weekly/ Calcutta	Tarachand Dutta and Bhabani Charan Bandopadhyay, Overseen by Raja Ram Mohan Roy.
1822	*Mumbaina Samachar* - Guajarati/ Bi-Weekly » Weekly » Daily in 1855 /Bombay Samachar (*MumbaiSamachar*)	Fardaonji Murzban.
1822	*Bangdoot*- Bangla/Hindi/Persian/ English/Journal	Editor-Neelratna Halda, Close associate of Raja Ram Mohan Roy.
1822	*Mirat-ul-Akbhar*- Persian/Weekly/ Calcutta	Raja Ram Mohan Roy.
1822	*Samachar Chandrika*-Bangla/Weekly/ Calcutta	Bhabani Charan Bandopadhyay
1826	*Udant Martand*-Hindi/ Weekly/ Calcutta	Jugal Kishore Shukla, 1st. Hindi Newspaper.

1838	*Bombay Times(and Journal of Commerce)*- English /Bi-Weekly » Daily/Bombay (Became Daily in 1850, 1861 onwards it became *Timesof India*)	JE Bernnan, Robert Knight* & Thomas Bennett,Indian ownership-Raibahadur Dinanath Velkar.
1843	*Tatvabodhini* - Bangla/ Journal/ Calcutta	D N Tagore and Akshay K. Dutta.
1845	*Benares Akhbar*- Hindi/Weekly/Benares	Raja Shivprasad Sitar-e-Hind.
1849	*Lahore Chronicle*-English/Weekly/Lahore	Syed Mohammed Azim.
1853	*Hindu Patriot*- English/weekly/Calcutta	Girish Chandra Ghosh,later HarishChandra Mukherjee.
1854	*Samachar Sudhavarshan*- Hindi/Daily/ Calcutta	Shyam Sunder Sen, 1*. Hindi Daily.
1854	*Rast Goftar*- Zoroastrian/ Fortnightly/ Bombay	Dadabhai Naoroji .
1855-56	Santal Hul or Uprising	} India's First War of
1857	Revolt of 1857 or the Sepoy Mutiny	} Independence
1857	*Payam-e-Azadi*- Hindi/Weekly/ Lucknow	Mirza Bahadur Bakht, Grand son ofBahadur Shah.
	On June 13, 1857, Act XV of 1857-	**Gagging Act**
1858	*Somprakash*- Bangla/Weekly/ Calcutta	Ishwar Chandra Vidyasagar, Ed. Dwarkanath Vidyabhushan.
1861	*Indian Mirror*- Bangla-English/ Fortnightly » Daily (From1871), Calcutta	Manmohan Ghosh & Devendra Nath Togore.
1865	*The Pioneer*- English/Allahabad/ Tri-Weekly » Daily, moved to Lucknow later	George Allen. Rudyard Kipling andWinston Churchill were associated with the paper; both won Nobel Prize in literature in 1907 and 1953respectively.
1866	*Indian public Opinion*-English/Daily/ Lahore, *Lahore Chronicle* Collapsed in 1867 and later purchased by *Indian Public opinion* and merged.	Civil Servants.
1866	*Akhbar-e-Chunar*- Urdu/weekly/ Chunar, UP	Balmukund Gupta.

	Press and Registration of Books Act of 1867	
1867	*Kavi Vachan Sudha*-Hindi/ Monthly»Weekly/Benaras	Bhartendu Harishchandra.
1868	*Amritbazar Patrika* - Bangla/Weekly/ Calcutta, Later became English Daily.	Sisir Kumar Ghosh, Motilal Ghosh.
1871	*Tehzib-e-Akhlaque*- Urdu./Journal/ Calcutta	Sir Sayed Ahmed Khan.
1872	*Bangdarshan*- Bangla/Weekly/Calcutta	Bankim Chandra Chatterjee/ Revived in 1901 By Ravindra Nath Tagore.
1872	*Civil and Military Gazette*-English/ Weekly/ Lahore, Simla, Karachi and Calcutta. It acquired *Agra Mofussilite* of Agra in 1876	Stephen Wheeler. This was Rudyard Kipling's first association with newspaper.
1872	*Behar Bandhu*-Hindi/Weekly/ Calcutta, shifted to Patna in 1874	Keshav Ram Bhatt and Munshi Hasan Ali.
1873	*Halishahar Patrika*- Anglo-Vernacular/ Journal/ Halishahar (24 Pargana, WB)	Kishori Mohan Ganguly.
1874	*Swadesh* - Hindi/Daily/Delhi	Lala Sriniwas Das.
1874	*Balbodhini*- Hindi/Women-Centric Magazine/Benaras	Bhartenu Harishchandra.
1875	*The Statesman(and the Friends ofIndia)*- English/Daily/Calcutta	Robert Knight.
1877	*Hindi Pradeep*- Hindi/Monthly / Allahabad	Balkrishna Bhatt.
	Act IX of 1878 - Vernacular Press Act	
1877	*Bharat Mitra*- Hindi/Weekly/Calcutta	Balmukumd Gupta.
1880	*Uchit Vakta*- Hindi/Weekly/Calcutta	Pt. Durga Prasad Mishra.
1878	*The Hindu*- English/Daily/Madras	Vir Raghavacharya and G.S. Aiyar.
	Newspaper Incitement of Offence Act	**1880**
1881	*The Tribune* Anglo-Vernacular bi-Weekly/Lahore, shifted to Ambala	Sirdar Dayal Singh Majithia assisted by Sir Surendra Nath Banerjee.
1881	*Dainik Basumati*/ Bangla/Weekly »Daily/ Calcutta	Upendranath Mukhopadhyay.
1881	*Kesari*- Marathi/ Weekly/Poona	Bal Gangadhar Tilak, V K Chiplunkar, Gopal Ganesh Agarkar.
1881	*Maratha*-Eng/ Weekly/ Poona	Bal Gangadhar Tilak.

1882	*Swadesamithran*- Tamil/ Weekly »Daily/ Madras	G Subramaniya Aiyar
1883	*Hindustan*-Hindi/Weekly »Daily, Kalakanker, UP	Madan Mohan Malviya, Balmukund Gupta, Under patronage of Raja Rampal Singh of Kalakanker.
1883	*Voice of India*- English /Weekly/ Bombay, Later merged into *Indian Spectator* with *Champion* in 1902	Dadabhai Naoroji .
	Telegraph Act, Section 5 - 1885	
1887	*Deepika* - Malayalam/Daily/Then also in English	Nidhirical Mannikathanar.
1887	*Sudharak*- Anglo-Marathi/ Poona, Nagpur	Gopal Ganesh Agarkar.
1888	*Malyalam Manorama* -Malayalam/ Daily/Kottayam	K Verghese Mappillai.
1889	Official Secrets Act (Revised)	
1890	*Sarva Hitaishi*- Hindi/Daily/Patna	Babu Mahavir Prasad.
1890	*Hindi Bangbasi*- Hindi/Weekly/ Calcutta	Pt. Amrit Lal Chakravarty, then Pt.Ambika Pd. Bajpai
1892	*New India*- English/Weekly/Calcutta	Bipin Chandra Pal
1894	*Behar Times*- Weekly» Bi-Weekly »Daily, it became *Beharee* in 1906	Mahesh Narain, Akhouri Basudeo Narain Sinha and then MaheshawarPrasad.
1896	*Prabuddha Bharat*-English/Monthly/ Madras, Later shifted to Mayawati in Uttarakhand	P Aiyyaswami on behest of Swami Vivekanand, Later edited bySwamis of Ramkrishna order.
	Post Office Act-Section 5 (a) to (d) 1898	
	Cr. P. C 124 (a), 153(a) 1898	
1899	*Udbodhan*- Bangla/Magazine/Calcutta	Swami Vivekanand
1900	*O Heraldo*- Portuguese/Weekly/ Panjim, Goa.	Alexandre Moniz Barbosa.
1900	*Chattigarh Mitra*-Hindi/Magazine/ Pendra Area , Chattisgarh	Pandit Madhav Sapre, with Vaman Rao Lakhe.
1903	*Indian Opinion*- English/Newspaper/ Natal Province, South Africa, Followed by editions in Tamil, Hindi and Gujarati.	M K Gandhi. After him his son Mani Lal Gandhi.

1905	*Vande Matram*- Bangla/Weekly/Calcutta	Bipin Chandra Pal, Subodh ChandraMallik, and later edited by Sri Aurobindo from 1906.
1905	*Indian Sociologist*- English/Journal/London, shifted to Paris in 1907	Shyamji Krishna Verma.
1906	*Jugantar Patrika*- Bangla/Daily/Calcutta	Barindra K. Ghosh, Avinash Bhattacharya, Bhupendra Datta.
1907	*Free Hindustan* –Vancouver, British Columbia, Canada	Tarak Nath Das.
1907	*Nrisingh*- Hindi/Monthly/Calcutta	Ambika Prasad Bajpai
1908	*Kesari*- Hindi/Daily/Poona	PanditMadhav Sapre, Dr. BalkrishnaShriram Munje.
1908	*Andhra Patrika*- Telugu/Weekly » Daily/ Various territories, fromMadras-1914	Kasinadhuni Nageshwar Rao.
1909	*The Leader*- English/Daily/Allahabad	Madan Mohan Malviya.
1909	*Karmayogi*- English/Fortnightly/ Calcutta	Sunder Lal.
1909	*Talwar*- Berlin	Bhikaji Cama and Birendra Nath Chattopadhyaya .
1910	*Bombay Chronicle* - English/Weekly/ Bombay	Feroz Shah Mehta and B G Horniman.
	Press Act of 1910	
1911	*The Hitvad* - English/ Daily/Nagpur	Gopal Krishna Gokhale.
1911	*Kerala Kaumudi* – Malayalam/Daily/ Trivandrum	C V Kunhinarayan.
1911	*Comrade*- English/Weekly/Calcutta,shifted to Delhi Later	Moulana Mohammad Ali Jauhar.
1912	*Al-Hilal*- Urdu/ Weekly/Calcutta	Abul Kalam Azad.
1912	*Al-Balagh*-Urdu/ Weekly/Calcutta	Abul Kalam Azad
1912	Division of Bengal, Bihar became aseparate state,	Jallianwalla bagh Maasecre on April13
1913	*Pratap*- Hindi/Daily/ Kanpur	Ganesh Shankar Vidyarthi
1913	*Ghadar*- Urdu/Gurumukhi, SanFrancisco, USA	Lala Hardayal (Urdu), Kartar SinghSarabha(Gurmukhi)and team of Ghadar.
1914	*Ghadar* – Hindi, San Francisco, USA,	Ghadar Team.
1914	*New India*- Eng/Daily/Adyar, Madras	Annie Besant, Theosophical Publishing House, Adyar.

1916	*Vishwamitra* - Hindi/Daily/Calcutta	Mulchand Agrawal.
1918	*The Searchlight* -English/Daily/Patna	Sir Syed Haidar Hussain.
1919	*Tarun Bharat*-Marathi/Daily/Belgaum	Baburao Thakur.
1919	*Navjeevan*- Gjarati/ Weekly » Daily/ Ahmadabad	M K Gandhi.
1919	*Young India* - English/Bi-Weekly/ Bombay	M K Gandhi.
1919	*Independent* -English/ Weekly »Daily/ Allahabad	Motilal Nehru and Syed Hussain.
1919	*The Samaj*- Oriya/Daily/Cuttack	Utkalmani Pandit, Gopabandhu Das.
1920	*Mooknayak*- Marathi/Fortnightly/ Bombay (Every alternate Saturday).	B R Ambedkar.
1920	*Desh*-Hindi/weekly/Patna	Babu Rajendra Prasad.
1920	*Aaj*- Hindi/ Daily/Banaras, UP	Shivprasad Gupta, Editors: Sriprakash and Baburao Vishnu Paradkar
1920	*Phulchhab*- Gujrati/Daily/Rajkot	Zaverchand Meghani, Amritlal Seth et al.
1920	*Swatantrata*- Hindi/Daily/Calcutta	Pt. Ambika Pd. Bajpai
1921	*Nava Kaal*- Marathi/Daily/Bombay	Krushnaji Khadilkar.
1922	*Anandbazaar Patrika*- Bangla/Daily/ Calcutta, Had its roots in Jessore (Bangladesh)	Tushar Kanti Ghosh and his fatherSisir Kanti Ghosh.
1923	*Matwala*-Hindi/Daily/Calcutta	Shivpujan Sahay, Munshi Navjadeek Lal shrivastva and Suryakant Tripathi Nirala
1923	*Sandesh*- Gujrati/Daily/Ahmadabad	Falgunibahi Patel.
1923	*Mathrubhumi*- Malayalam Daily/ Kozhikode	K P Kesava Menon.
1923	*Hindustan Times*- Delhi/English/Daily	Sunder Singh Layalpuri / K.M. Pannikar
1924	Daily *Aikya*- Marathi/ Weekly »/Daily/ Satara	Shri Raobahdur Kale.
1927	*The Musalman*- Urdu/Daily/Madras	Syed Azmatullah.
1927	*Bahishkrit Bharat*-Marathi/ Fortnightly/Bombay	B R Ambedkar
1927	*The Free Press Journal* - English/ Daily/ Bombay	Swaminathan Sadanand.

1929	*Vishal Bharat*-Hindi/Magzine/Calcutta	Banarasidas Chaturvedi, Ramanand Chattopahyaya
1931	*The Indian Express*- English/Daily/ Bombay and from various territories.	Ramnath Goenka. In 1936 he bought a majority stake from S. Sadanand.
1931	*The Indian Nation*- English/Daily/Patna	Sri Kameshwar Singh, Ed. Nevile Vimant(of London Times)
1932	*Gujarat Samachar*-Gujarati/Daily/ Ahmadabad	Shantilal Shah
1932	*Sakal*- Marathi/ Daily/Poona	Dr. N P a.k.a Namsaheb Parulekar.
1932	*Harijan(Eng)Harijan Bandhu(Guj), Harijan Sevak (Hindi)* -Weekly	M K Gandhi.
1933	*Dinamani*-Tamil/Daily/Madras	A N Sivaraman.
1933	*Bharat*- Hindi/Bi-Weekly/Allahabad	Nand Dulare Bajpai
1934	*Chandrika*-Malayalam/Daily/Thalassery, Kozhikode	Chief editor-C H Mohammed Koya,Former Kerala CM.
1935	*Tamil Murasu*-Tamil/Daily/Singapore	Thamizhavel G. Sarangpani.
1936	*Hindustan* Daily-Hindi/Daily/Delhi	Madan Mohan Malviya
1936	*Dainik Navajyoti*- Daily/Hindi/Ajmer	Capt. Durga Prasad Choudhary
1937	*Navbharat*- Daily/Hindi/Nagpur	Ramgopal Maheshwari
1938	*National Herald*- English/Daily/Lucknow	Jawahar Lal Nehru.
1938	*Deccan Chronicle*-Daily/English/ Hyderabad	Rajgopal Mudliyar
1938	*Andhra Prabha*-Telugu/Daily/Hyderabad	Ramnath Goenka, Ed-Mootha Gautham.
1939	*Assam Tribune*- English/ Weekly » Daily /Gauhati	Radhagovind Baruah .
1941	*The Dawn* - English/ Weekly » Daily (1944) /Delhi, Shifted to Karachi in 1947	Mohammad Ali Jinnah.
1941	*Ajit*- Gurumukhi, Jalandhar. Started as Urdu weekly from Lahore, Shifted to India after independence and language changed to Gurumukhi and it became Daily	Ajit Singh Ambalvi, Sandhu Singh Hamdard.
1941	*Aryawarta*- Hindi /Daily/Patna	Dinanath jha, Braj Nandan Azad.

1942	*Dainik Jagaran*- Hindi/Daily/Kanpur	Pawanchandra Gupta, and NarendraMohan.
1942	*Deshabhimani*- Malayalam/Daily/Calicut	EMS Namboodripad, Now ownedby Kerala State Committee of CPI(M).
1942	*Prajashakti*- Telugu / Weekly »Dailyfrom 1945/Vijayawada	F- CPI(M), Ed-Mallayosyuala Venkat Subrahmaniyam Sarma.
1945	*The Shillong Times*, English Tabloid Weekly »Daily/Shillong	Patricia Mukhim.
1946	*Sanmarg* - Hindi/Daily/Calcutta	Swami Karpatri Ji.
1947	*Nai Duniya*-Hindi/Daily/Indore	Labhchand Chhajlani and Basanti Lal Sethia.
1947	*Navbharat Times*- Hindi/Daily/Delhi	Times of India Group, Akshay Kumar Jain
1947	*Pradeep- Hindi/Daily/Patna*	Radheshyam Sharma

» Later became

* Robert Knight: Out of need and making both end meet for his large family, Robert Knight started contributing to newspapers. Luck got him in the seat of the vacationing editor of Bombay Times. He never looked back and laid the foundation for another great paper in Calcutta The Statesman.

* James silk Buckingham: More than any single person he tirelessly campaigned against the restriction and censorship imposed on the press in his times.

In 1766, William Bolts, a Dutchman, proposed to start a printing press in Calcutta. But he was not only refused permission but he was also deported.

The Baptist missionaries of Serampore, were the forerunner to initiate the publication of newspapers and magazines in Bangla.

There were remarkable publications that enriched Indian writings in more ways than one. Pandit Madhav Sapre was an institution in himself. He wrote first story in Hindi, *Tokri Bhar Mitti* . He translated *Abhigyan Shakuntalam* of Kalidasa and *Ramcharitmanas* of Tulsidsa into Hindi and laid foundation of *Chattisgarh Mitra* and *Karmveer*.

Hindi publication Saraswati (Founded-Chintamani Ghosh, Edited by Pt Mahavir Prasad Dwivedi-1903) successfully carried out work of giving Hindi a standard format. Dwivedi Ji freed Hindi from the influence of Brajbhasha, Avadhi, and different dialectal influences that paved the way for Khadi Boli a precursor of modern Hindi. He was the mentor of Maithili Sharan Gupta, Kashi Prasad Jaiswal, and Ganesh Shankar Vidyarthi.

Special issues like Vijay Ank of Swadesh, Phansi Ank of Chand, Jhanda Satyagraha Ank of Prabha are compilations of historical importance. Ghadar di Goonj, a special issue of Ghadar containing a collection of folk patriotic songs was reprinted on the reader's demand.

Some extraordinary contributions from English journalists helped in bringing scientific interest within the purview of journalism. The Asiatic Society (founded in 1784 by Sir William Johns) had been publishing papers related to Zoology, Botany, Geology, Chemistry, Physics, Anthropology, Meteorology, and Medicine. *The Journal of Asiatic Society* incorporated the publication named Gleanings in Science, three volumes of which were published during 1829–1831. Subsequently, the Indian Review and Journal of Foreign Science, which was published in 8 volumes between 1834–1847, were also incorporated in the *Journal of the Asiatic Society.*

Kishori Mohan Ganguli published Halishahar Patrika, in which he translated Mahabharata into English.

Appendix IV: List of People Who Also Made News

Mangal Pandey, Vazir Ali Khan, Basudeo Balwant Phadke, Daulat Rao Dware, Krishnaji Pant Gogate, Shyamji, Krishna Verma, Damodar Chapekar, Balkrishna Chaphekar, Laxmibai, Nanasahab, Vinayak Damodar Savarkar, Lala Hardayal, Lala Lajpat Roy, Pandurang Mahadeo Vapat, Vasudeo Chapekar, Virendra Kumar Ghosh, Madan Lal Dhingra, Lokmanya Tilak, Gyanchandra Verma, Ganesh Savarkar, Kore Gaokar, Anant Kenhre, Krishnaji Keshav Karve, Vinayak Deshpande, Sardar Bhagat Singh, Arvind Ghosh, Hemchandra Das, Khudiram Bose, Prafulla Chaki, Upendra Nath Banerjee, Ullaskar Dutta, Narendra Goswami, Satyendra Chaki, Rasbihari Bose, Master Ameerchand, Hanumant Sahay, Kanhaiya Lal Dutta, Avadh Behari, Ganeshi Lal, Sachindra Nath Sanyal, Bhupendra Nath Dutta, Damodar Swaroop Seth, Suresh Chandra Bhattacharya, Dinanath, Vasant Kumar Vishwas, Balmukund, Balraj Bhalla, Kartar Singh Sarabha, Vissnu Govind Pingley, Jitendra Sanyal, Ravindra Sanyal, Bhupendra Nath Sanyal, Kaple, Heramb Lal Gupta, D.S. Deshpande, Subhash Chandra Bose, Sardar Ajit Singh, Bhai Permanand, J.N. Chatterjee, Pandurag Sadasheo, Adharchand Laskar, Surendra Mohan Bose, Girin Mukherjee, Baba Sohan Singh Bakhna, Baba Kesar Singh, Kashiram, Mathura Singh, Balwant Singh, Arun Singh, Uttam Singh, Jeevan Singh, Manvendra Nath Roy, Gendalal Dixit, Ganesh Shankar Vidyarthi, Ramprasad Bismil, Shivakrishna, Bholanath Chattopadhyaya, Yatindra Nath Mukherjee, Shripat Amrit Dange, Shaukat Usmani, Ashfaque ulla Khan, Roshan Singh, Prem Krishna

Khanna, Rajendra Nath Lahiri, Vidhnu Sharan Dublis, Shachindra Nath Buxi, Keshav Chakrabarthy, Murari Lal, Manmath Nath Gupta,Yogesh Chandra Chatterjee, Govindcharan Kar, Raj Kumar Singh, Ramkrishna Khatri, Ram Dulare Deviwadi, Yatindra Nath Das, Manindra Banerjee, Ramesh Chandra Gupta, Yashpal, Ram Rakha, Mahavir Singh, Namdas, Mohitmohan Maitra, Sukhdeo, Rajguru, Shivram, Batukeshwar Dutt, Kundanlal, Vijay Kumar, Jaideo Kapoor, Swarna Singh, Bhagwati Charan Verma, Jaichandra Vidhyalankar, Gopi Mohan Saha, Surendra Pandey, Jaigopal, Kishori Lal, Vijay Kumar Sinha, Shiv Verma, Gaya Prasad, Kamalnath Tewari, Aasharam, Deshraj, Premdutt, Markandeya, Manmohan Gupta, Harendra Bhattacharya, Ram Narayan Mishra, Mahendra Choudhary, Phulena Prasad, Matangini Hazra, Kaushalya Kumar, Chitta Pandey, Suryanath Upadhyay, Kanaklata Barua, Mukund Kabta, Laxmidas, Ramchandra Bera, Satishchandra Samant, Parshuram, Siyaram, Yogendra Shukla, Uttamchand, Ramanand Mishra, Maganlal Bagri, Syamlal Nayak, Hemuphalani, Nana Patil, Udham Singh, Sarkar Shardul Singh, Rahmat Khan, Gaya Munda, Birsa Munda, Singi daiee, Thakur Vishwanath Shahdeo, Pandey Ganpat Roy, Neelambar-Peetambar,Sido- Kanhu, Tilka Manjhi… The list is endless…

(*List was compiled by Dr. Kusheshwar Thakur for Swatantra Sangram Visheshank-2 of* Brahmarshi Samaj Darshan, *edited by Dhrmaraj Roy, July–Sept.2014, published from Ranchi*).

References

Chapter 1: Role of Science and technology in rise and growth ofmass media and communication in India.

1. Heather Whips-How the Hyoid Bone Changed History, February 03, 2008

   URL: http://www.livescience and technology.com/7468-hyoid-bone-changed-history.html

2. Ibid

3. Nature Online-Natural History Museum, URL:http://www. nhm. ac.uk/nature-online/life/human- origins/early human-family/ homo-heidelbergensis/index.html

4. Bernal, Martin Black Athena-The Afroasiatic Roots of Classical Civilization.Introduction. http://rhetrepository.wordpress. com/2008/02/23/r-t-oliver-communication-and-culture-in-ancient-india-and-china/

5. History of writing-livescience and technology.com: URL: http:// www.livescience and technology.com/7468-writing-changed-history.html

6. Also see, Gray, Elizabeth-Story of Journalism Longmans Young Book. UK., 1968, p4

7. How writing Changed History-livescience and technology. com, URL: http://www.livescience and technology.com/

7468-writing- changed-history.html, also see Story of Journalism by Gray, Elizabeth, Longmans Young Book, UK 1968, p5

8-9. Ibid

10. Gray, Elizabeth-Story of Journalism, Longmans Young Book, UK 1968, p4.

11. Encyclopedia Britannica, https://www.britannica.com/topic/Semitic-languages

12. Gray, Elizabeth-Story of Journalism (1968),Longmans Young Book UK .p4

13. Aramean Democratic Organization- The Material Used for Writing in Ancient Time, URL: http://www.aramaic-dem.org/English/ politik/112.html

14. Gray, Elizabeth-Story of Journalism Longmans Young Book, UK, 1968, p4

15. Ibid

16. University Of Michigan -Ancient Writing Materials: Papyrus URL:http://www.lib.umich.edu/papyrology-collection/ancient-writing-materials-papyrus Papyrus fragment with lines from Homer's Odyssey, Gift of Egypt Exploration Fund, 1909

17. Ibid

18. Gift of Egypt Exploration Fund (1909)-Heilbrunn Timeline of Art History. URL: http://www.metmuseum.org/toah/works-of-art/09.182.50

19-20. Ibid.

21. Gray, Elizabeth-Story of Journalism Longmans Young Book, UK 1968, p2

22. Encyclopedia Britannica @britannica.com/

23. Encyclopedia Iranica URL: http://www.iranicaonline.org/ articles/ gandhari-language

24. Dr. Schadler, Kenneth – The Origin of Vedic Civilization the Flow of Science and technologies and Mathematics from India to Arabia and Europe. URL :http:vamdevananda.wordpress.com/tag/flow of science and technology and mathematics

25. Hoberman, Barry- *The Battle of Talas,* Saudi Aramco World, pp. 26-31 (Sept/Oct 1982), https//archive.aramcoworld.com/1983/ the battle of talas

26. Domino, Michael- Professor of IIT, Gandhinagar, *The Times of India*, Print Edition, February 9,2015.

27. Gray, *Elizabeth -Story of Journalism* Longmans Young Book, UK,1968 , p7.

28. Stein, Aurel-*A Chinese Expedition across the Pamir and Hindukush*, A.D. 747, The Geographic Journal, 59:2, Feb. 1922, pp. 112-131

29. Gernet, Jacque, Foster, J. R. (trans.), Charles Hartman (trans.)-*A History of Chinese Civilization* 1996.

30. Ibid

Mass Media in the Beginning:

1. Constable and Smith, Eds- Travels in the Mogul Empire- p.231, Undated, http://www.columbia.edu/cu/lweb/digital/collections/cul/texts/ldpd_6093710_000/

2. Manucci,Niccola,-Storia de Mogor, pp-331-332, https://archive.org/ details/storiadomogororm01manuuoft

   Also see: H. Baveridge's review in the Journal of Royal Asiatic Society, October, 1908. "As stated by him, in 1828 Colonel James Tod sent some hundreds of original manuscript newspapers of the Mogul Court (1660) to the Royal Asiatic Society in London. These papers were 8 inches by 4 inches in size on an average and were of course, written in various hands. They record notices of promotions, visits by the Emperor of mosques and shrines, hunting expeditions, the bestowal of presents and items of news of similar interest"

3. Barns, Margarita, The Indian press, 1940, p 4
4. Ibid
5. Sleeman,William-Ramblesand Recollections, 1844, p. 249, https:// archive.org/details/ramblesrecollect01sleeuoft/page/x/mode/2up
6. Sleeman, William-Journey through the Kingdom of Oude, Vol I, pp 67- 69. https://archive.org/details/jeanjacquesrouss02macd
7. The Calcutta Review, Vol.CXXIV (1907) pp. 355-58, Also see Barns Margarita: op. cit., pp 32-33.
8. Barns, Margarita-The Indian press, 1940, p 5

Gutenberg's Remarkable Machine and Thereafter:

1. Gray, Elizabeth, *The Story of Journalism*, Longmans Young Book, UK, 1968 p 5
2. *Ibid.*
3. Hutter David-*1001 Inventions That Changed The World*, Hachette Book Publishing India Pvt. Ltd. Edition published by Hachette India, 2013 p 177
4. Fricker, Margaret-*1001 Inventions That Changed The World*, Hachette Book Publishing India Pvt. Ltd. published by Hachette India, 2013, p 164

5-6. *Ibid*

7. Livescience and technology.com: *How Printing Changed History*, http://www.livescience and technology.com/7468- how printing changed history.

8. *Ibid*

9. *Ibid, also see* Hutter David-*1001 Inventions That Changed The World*, Hachette Book Publishing India Pvt. Ltd. Edition published by Hachette India, 2013 p177

10. Kennedy, Susan-*1001 Inventions That Changed The World*, Hachette Book Publishing India Pvt. Ltd. Edition published by Hachette India, 2013,p 240

11. Encyclopedia Britannica @ *britannica.com*

12. Baldwin, Tamara Kay-*The Function of newspaper in Society: A Global Perspective, Ed* ,Shannon E. Martin & David A Copeland, Praeger Publications, US, 2003, p 89

13. Ibid

14. Shanon E. Martin-*newspaper History Tradition*, The *Function of newspaper in Society: A Global Perspective, Ed* , Shannon E. Martin & David A Copeland, Praeger Publications, US, 2003 p1

15. Curt, Buhker *The Fifteenth Century Book: The Scribes, The Printers, The decorators*, University of Pennsylvania, US ,1960 as quoted in *The Function of newspaper in Society*: A Global Perspective, *Ed*, Shannon E. Martin & David A Copeland, Praeger Publications, US, 2003 p 89 [For the Argument see: Eisenstein, Elizabeth: *The Printing press as an Agent of Change: Communication and Cultural Transformation in Early Modern Europe*, Cambridge University press, London.]

16. Pearce, Robert: *1001 Inventions That Changed The World*, Hachette Book Publishing India Pvt. Ltd. Edition published by Hachette India, 2013 p 274,Also see: *The History of The World*

in 366 Days, Octopus Publishing Group, 1992 Revised and Updated edition by Hachette India, 2015, p18 Feb.

17. Ibid
18. The Economist: Special Holiday Double Issue, Social Media of 16th. Century, How Luther went viral, December 17-30,2011, p 84.
19. Livescience.com on its site as mentioned above.
20. Gray, Elizabeth: *The Story of Journalism*, Longmans Young Book, UK, 1968 p 6
21. Hutter David:*1001 Inventions That Changed The World*, Hachette Book Publishing India Pvt. Ltd. Edition published by Hachette India, 2013, p 177
22. Bond, Richard: *Inventions That Changed The World*, Hachette Book Publishing India Pvt. Ltd. Edition published by Hachette India, 2013, p 177
23. *Ibid*
24. Gray, Elizabeth: *The Story of Journalism*, Longmans Young Book, UK, 1968 p. 50
25. James Grant: *1001 Inventions That Changed The World*, Hachette Book Publishing India Pvt. Ltd. Edition published by Hachette India, 2013,p177
26. James Grant: op. cit., p 336
27. Barns, Margarita: *The Indian press*, 1940, p 181
28. Kumar, N- *Ed. Journalism in Bihar*, Government of Bihar, Supplement to Bihar Gazette, Gazetteers Branch, Revenue Department, Patna,1971p.33
29. Barns, Margarita: op.cit., p230

30. Kumar, N: op.cit., p 230

31. Indian press Commission Report, II: https://books.google. co.in/books/about/Report_of_the_Second_Press_Commission.html?id=LWMoAQAAMAAJ&redir_esc=y *32-33 Ibid*

Chapter 2: Role of Media in national movement leading to independence

1. Kumar, N- State Editor, Bihar District Gazetteers, A supplement to Bihar State Gazetteer, Government of Bihar, Gazetteers Branch, Revenue Department, Patna, 1971. p9

2. As it is evident in the copy of Hicky's Gazeette preserved in Heidelberg University, Germany.

3. Kumar, N State Editor, Bihar District Gazetteers, A supplement to Bihar State Gazetteer, Government of Bihar, Gazetteers Branch, Revenue Department, Patna, 1971. p10

4. See copy of Hicky's Gazette preserved in Heidelberg University, Germany.

   Kumar, N- State Editor, Bihar District Gazetteers, A supplement to Bihar State Gazetteer, Government of Bihar, Gazetteers Branch, Revenue Department,Patna,1971. pp 10-12

7-9. *Ibid*

10. Hickey, William: *Memoirs of William Hickey*, Vol III pp. 160-161 (Hickey was a contemporary attorney practicing in Bengal.) https://books.google.co.in/books?id=hwUxjibjPYEC&redir_esc=y

11. Kumar N State Editor, Bihar District Gazetteers, A supplement to Bihar State Gazetteer, Government of Bihar, Gazetteers Branch, Revenue Department, Patna, 1971. p. 13

12. Gray, Elizabeth: The Story of Journalism, Longman Young Book, UK,1968 p 30

13. *Ibid*

14. Barns, Margarita: *The Indian press*,1940, p 53

15. Kumar, N : State Editor, Bihar District Gazetteers, A supplement to Bihar State Gazetteer, Government of Bihar, Gazetteers Branch, Revenue Department, Patna, 1971, p 20.

16. Barns, Margarita: *The Indian press*,1940, p55

17. Kumar, N : State Editor, Bihar District Gazetteers, A supplement to Bihar State Gazetteer, Government of Bihar, Gazetteers Branch, Revenue Department,Patna,1971,p 20. *op. cit.*, pp 13-14

18. *Ibid*

19. Barns, Margarita: *The Indian press* p56 https://archive.org/details/ dli.ernet.6202

20-21 *Ibid*

22. Kumar, N : State Editor, Bihar District Gazetteers, A supplement to Bihar State Gazetteer, Government of Bihar, Gazetteers Branch, Revenue Department,Patna,1971,p 20. op.cit., p17, also see Barns Margarita, p56

23. *Ibid*

24. Hill, James: *History of British India*, Vol. III, 1846,p58

25. Historical MSS. Commission: *Manuscript of F. B. Forteqcue*, Esqr., Vol. IV, p. 383. Also see, Margarita Barns: op. cit., p. 73. -25

26. Kumar, N: State Editor, Bihar District Gazetteers, A supplement to Bihar State Gazetteer, Government of Bihar, Gazetteers Branch, Revenue Department, Patna,1971, p 20.

27. Barns, Margarita: *The Indian press*, 1940, p 95

28. *Ibid* p 96

29. Kumar, N State Editor, Bihar District Gazetteers, A supplement to BiharState Gazetteer, Government of Bihar, Gazetteers Branch, Revenue Department, Patna,1971.p 26

30. Barns, Margarita: *op.cit.*,p 95

31. Kumar, N: State Editor, Bihar District Gazetteers, A supplement to Bihar State Gazetteer, Government of Bihar, Gazetteers Branch, Revenue Department, Patna,1971. p 28

32-33. *Ibid*

34. Choudhary, Reba:The Sory of Indian press, The Economic Weekly, Feb,26, 1995, p 291

35. Kumar, N: *op.cit.* p 30

36. Encyclopedia britannica:@britannica.com

37. *Indian newspaper Reports*, c1868-1942 in the BritishLibrary, London. Preserved digitally on Library site.

38. Barns, Margariata: The Indian press, 1940 p 299

39. Kumar,N: State Editor, Bihar District Gazetteers, A supplement to Bihar State Gazetteer, Government of Bihar, Gazetteers Branch, Revenue Department, Patna, 1971pp32-34

40. *Ibid*

41. Dr. Sharma, Shankar Dayal – Jhabar Mall Sharma Memorial Lecture at Jaipur. Pundit Jhabar Mall Sharma was a noted journalist and writer from Rajasthan. A lecture in his memory was organized every year by Makhan Lal Chaturvedi Patrakarita Vishwavidyalaya (Now Makhan Lal Chaturvedi University of Journalism and Mass Communication). The first lecture in the series was delivered by D. Shankar Dayal Sharma (then) the President of India, on January 4, 1992 at Jaipur in which I was

present as Deputy Resident Editor of Navbharat Times, Jaipur. A copy of the lecture is available with me and was later published in Brahamarshi Samaj Darshan (special issue on Independence) July–Sept. 2013.The subject of the lecture was *Swatantrata Andolan Men Hindi Patrakarita Ka Yogdan* (contribution of Hindi journalism in Independence movement).

42. Kumar, N: State Editor, Bihar District Gazetteers, A supplement to Bihar State Gazetteer, Government of Bihar, Gazetteers Branch, Revenue Department, Patna, 1971.

43. Dr. Sharma, Shankar Dayal – Jhabar Mall Sharma Memorial Lecture at Jaipur.

44-45. Ibid

46. Dr. Sharma, Shankar Dayal – Jhabar Mall Sharma Memorial Lecture at Jaipur.

47-48. *Ibid*

49. Indian Newspaper Reports, c1868-1942 in the British Library, London. Preserved digitally on Library site:

    http://www.ampltd.co.uk/digital_guides/indian_newspaper_reports_parts_1_to_4/Publishers-Note-Part-6.aspx

50. Dr. Sharma, Shankar Dayal – Jhabar Mall Sharma Memorial Lecture at *.Ibid*

51. Chaturvedi, Jagdish Prasad- Role of in India's Struggle for Freedom, All India Congress Committee site Chaturvedi Jagdish Prasad – Role of press in India's Freedom Struggle. Site of All India Congress Committee @ http://aicc.org.in/web.php/history/detail/17

52. Dr. Sharma, Shankar Dayal – Jhabar Mall Sharma Memorial Lecture at Jaipur,

53-57. *Ibid*

58. Indian Newspaper Reports, c1868-1942 in the British Library, London. Preserved digitally on Library site. http://www.ampltd.co.uk/digital_guides/indian_newspaper_reports_parts_1_to_4/ Publishers-Note-Part-6.aspx

59. Gandhi, M K -Picture of Free India p. 211

60. Dr. Sharma, Shankar Dayal – Jhabar Mall Sharma Memorial Lecture at Jaipur

61. Bhaskar,Vijay-Bihar Men Parakarita ka Itihas, Prabhat Prakashan, New Delhi 2013 pp. 47-51.

62. Dr. Sharma, Shankar Dayal – Jhabar Mall Sharma Memorial Lecture at Jaipur.

63-66. *Ibid*

67. Singh, Vipul-*Longman History & Civics*, p-33

68.-69. *Ibid*

70. Dr. Sharma, Shankar Dayal – Jhabar Mall Sharma Memorial Lecture at Jaipur.

71-72. *Ibid*

73. Indian newspaper Reports, c1868-1942 in the British Library, London. Preserved digitally on Library site.

74. *The Searchlight* October 26, 1921.

75. Edwin S. Montagu, An Indian Diary, London, 1930 p-8. https://archive.org/details/AnIndianDiary

76. Dr. Shrivasta, NMP: History of the Searchlight Daily- Kashi Prasad Jaiswal Research Institute, Patna, 1998. p-124

77. *Ibid*

78. Kumar, N: State Editor, Bihar District Gazetteers, A Supplement, Govt. of Bihar, Gazetteers Branch, Revenue Department, Patna,1971. p-46.

79. Pundit Bajpai, Ambika Prasad- *Samachar Patron Ka Itihas* p-215.

80. Kumar, N: State Editor, Bihar District Gazetteers, A Supplement, Govt. of Bihar, Gazetteers Branch, Revenue Department, Patna,1971. p.108

81. Dr. Mishra, Krishna Behari- *Hindi Patrakarita*, 1968,p.319.

82. Kumar, N: State Editor, Bihar District Gazetteers, A Supplement, Govt. of Bihar, Gazetteers Branch, Revenue Department, Patna,1971. p-47

83. Gurmel S. Sidhu, Professor California State University, Fresno, California-*Ghadar Movement: Role of Media and Literature* p-.1

84. The Ghadar Movement: How it gained momentum in the USA – Literature of Ghadar Movement- Digitally preserved on Ghadar Heritage foundation site at http://Ghadar.homestead.com/ GhadarHist.html. Also see sikhwiki.org.php./Ghadar.party

85. 'Vatuk' Ved Prakash- Ghadar Andolan America se Shuroo Hua Tha- Kadambini-October 1997.Former Professor, Ved Vatuk, of Berkley, has collected all the original issue of " Ghadar" published in Punjabi during 1913-1914, and photo copied them and put them together in a book form. Ghadar Party da Saptahik Parcha (Bhag pehla, 1913-1914. Folklore Institute, Berkley, California.2010, Pages-354.

86. Gurmel S. Sidhu, Professor California State University, Fresno, California-*Ghadar Movement: Role of Media and Literature* p-6.

87-89. *Ibid*

90. Prof. Lal, Chaman, Jawahal Nehru University, *The Hindu*, August 12, 2013

91. 'Vatuk' Ved Prakash-Ghadar Andolan America se Shuroo Hua Tha- Kadambini-October 1997

92. *An article translated from Punjabi and originally written by Sardar Bhagat Singh, published in Ghadar, a Newsletter of the Ghadar Memorial Center, 5 Wood Street, San Francisco, CA 94117 November/December 1992*

93. Prof. Lal, Chaman, Jawaharlal Nehru University, *The Hindu*, August 12, 2013

94. *Director of the Intelligence Bureau, Home Department, New Delhi 1934*

95. *Account of Ghadar Conspiracy Punjab Police, Lahore 1919*

96. *(94 & 95)* As documented *in* History of Ghadar Movement by Jaspal Singh under *British View on Ghadar*)

97. Chaturvedi Jagdish Prasad – Role of press in India's Freedom Struggle. Site of All India Congress Committee @ http://aicc. org. in/web.php/history/detail/17

Chapter 3: Role of Gandhi in development of journalism in India;

1. Guha, Ramchandra- *Gandhi, the journalist*, Hindu, Online edition of India's National newspaper, Jun 08, 2003, http://ramachandraguha. in/archives/gandhi-the-journalist-the-hindu.html

2-3. *Ibid*

4. Guha, Ramchandra *Gandhi the journalist* www.thehindu.com/ thehindu/mag/2003/06/.../2003060800320300.html

5. Kar, Souribandhu *Mahatma Gandhi:The Editor & Journalist* Odisha Review, October – 2012, p 35

6. Guha, Ramchandra- *Gandhi, the journalist*, Hindu, Online edition of India's National newspaper, Jun 08, 2003, www. thehindu.com/ thehindu/mag/2003/06/.../2003060800320300. html

7. *Ibid*

8. DrSharma, Shankar Dayal, Former President of India, Jhabarmall Sharma 1st Memorial Lecture at Jaipur .1992

9. *Ibid*

10. Chatterjee Sailen- *Reporting Mahatma* he had written for the special issue of Vidura on, *Gandhi as a Journalist* , Vidura, Jan-March, 1998

11. *Gupta, V S – Mahatma Gandhi and Mass Media, Employment News, Dated -29 September-5 October 2001, Vol. XXVI*

12. *Ibid*

13. Kar , Souribandhu *Mahatma Gandhi:The Editor & Journalist* Odisha Review, October – 2012, p 35 http://magazines.odisha. gov. in/Orissareview/2012/oct/engpdf/35-37.pdf

14. Gupta, V S – *Mahatma Gandhi and Mass Media, Employment News, Dated - 29 September-5 October 2001, Vol. XXVI*

15. *Ibid*

16. Kamath, M V- *Journalist Gandhi*(*Selected Writings of Gandhi*) First Edition, Gandhi Book Center, Bombay Sarvodaya Mandal, Mumbai, In Preface to the book compiled by Sunil Sharma *Journalist Gandhi*(*Selected Writings of Gandhi*) First Edition , 1994, p2

17. Raju, Chalpati as quoted in *Mahatma Gandhi and Mass Media, Employment News, Dated -29 September-5 October 2001, Vol. XXVI*

Chapter 4: Role of Media with Special Reference to newspapers1780-1980

1. Kumar, N: Bengal press in Nineteenth Century, Supplement to Bihar District Gazetteer, Journalism in Bihar, Govt. of Bihar, Gazetteer Branch, Revenue Deptt. Patna, 1971 p35
2. *Ibid.*
3. Barns, Margrita: The Indian press, 1940, p 189
4. Ruling the Wave: Economist, Special Holiday Double Issue, p 201
5. *Ibid.*
6. Dr. Sharma Shankar Dayal: Jhabar Mall Sharma, 1st Memorial Lecture at Jaipur, 1992
7. Kumar, N: op.cit pp 14-15
8. Memoirs of William Hickey: Vol. III pp. 160-161. (A cotemporary Practicing Attorney in Bengal)
9. Kumar, N: Bengal press in Nineteenth Century, Supplement to Bihar District Gazetteer, Journalism in Bihar, Govt. of Bihar, Gazetteer Branch, Revenue Deptt. Patna, 1971p35op. cit., p16
10. Hirschman, Edwin, Biographer of Robert Knight- The Reformist Editor,

11-12. *Ibid*

13. Kumar, N: Bengal press in Nineteenth Century, Supplement to Bihar District Gazetteer,Journalism in Bihar, Govt. of Bihar, Gazetteer Branch, Revenue Deptt. Patna, 1971 p 35

14. *Ibid*

15. Indian press Commission Report.

16. Encyclopedia Britannica, netedition: http//www.britannica.com

17. Kumar, N: Bengal press in Nineteenth Century, Supplement to Bihar District Gazetteer, Journalism in Bihar, Govt. of Bihar, Gazetteer Branch, Revenue Deptt. Patna, 1971p35op. cit., p16

18-19. *Ibid*

20. Barns, Margarita: op. cit., p16

21. Kumar, N : Bengal press in Nineteenth Century, Supplement to Bihar District Gazetteer, Journalism in Bihar, Govt. of Bihar, Gazetteer Branch, Revenue Deptt. Patna, 1971p35p 17

22. Barns Margrita: op. cit., p25

23. Chatterjee, Mrinal: The Pioneer 150 Years and going strong, Communication Today, Ed. Sanjeev Bhanavat, April-June 2014 pp110-113.ISSN 0975.217 X

24-25. *Ibid*

26. Indian newspaper Reports

27. Chatterjee, Mrinal: *Ibid*

28. Dr. Shrivastva, NMP: History of Searchlight Daily, Kashi Prasad Jaiswal Institute Research Institute, Patna,1988, p.

29. The Searchlight, July 25, 1920.p.133

30. Dr. NMP Shrivastva: History of Searchlight Daily, Kashi PrasadJaiswal Institute Research Institute, Patna,1988, *op.cit.*, p.132

Emergency: When democracy was wounded

1. Dr. Shrivastva, NMP: History of Searchlight Daily, Kashi Prasad Jaiswal Institute Research Institute,Patna,1988, p.463
2. Dr. Shrivastva, NMP: History of Searchlight Daily, Kashi Prasad Jaiswal Institute Research Institute,Patna,1988, p 48
3. Press Council's observation is for the *Searchlight* is recorded on pp 449-and for *Pradeep* on pp 457-461.
4. Ibid.
5. Narsimhan, VK: *Legalizing Ethics* The Indian Express, 6, June, 1977.
6. Aiyar, S P, Raju, S V: *When the Wind Blows: India's Ballot Box Revolution*, pp191-192. Also see Second press Commission Report in which entire correspondence between B G Verghese and K K Birla has been appendixed
7. *Ibid.*
8. Narsimhan, V K : *Democracy Redeemed*, S Chand New Delhi,1977, p 23
9. Aiyar, S P, Raju, S V: *When the Wind Blows: India's Ballot Box Revolution*, pp191-192 *op. cit.*, p 191

10-11. *Ibid* , p 193

12. Ibid, Also see Second press Commission Report where all eight big media business houses have been found not having interest confined to Media only.(A list of Big, Medium and Small newspaper Houses is in Appendix II).
13. Aiyar, S P, Raju, S V: *When the Wind Blows: India's Ballot Box Revolution* p 47

14. Aiyar, S P, Raju, S V: *When the Wind Blows: India's Ballot Box Revolution* p 29

15. Patwari, DP: Bhumiputra Case, Ahmedabad, Navjeevan press,1976.

16. Aiyar, S P, Raju, S V: *When the Wind Blows: India's Ballot Box Revolution*, *op. cit.*, p 205 (For Sunder Rajan, K R- *How Times of India Sold Out*, see Debonair, Bombay Vol. VI No. 6, June, 1977. For more on emergency also see *Syah se Syahi ka Sangharsh* in Bihar Men Patrkarita ka Itihas by Vijay Bhaskar, Prabhat Prakashan, Delhi 2013).

Index

T

U

V

W

X

Y

Z

www.ingramcontent.com/pod-product-compliance
Ingram Content Group UK Ltd.
Pitfield, Milton Keynes, MK11 3LW, UK
UKHW062311290726
14090UKWH00018B/995